Web.
Write.
Sell.

Write Ads, Headlines, and Calls to Action That People Can't Help But Click

Chris Kennedy

Questing Vole Press

Web. Write. Sell.: Write Ads, Headlines, and Calls to Action That People Can't Help But Click
by Chris Kennedy

Editor: Zack Diston
Proofreader: Diane Yee
Compositor: Sylvia Thorpe
Cover: Questing Vole Press

Contents

1   Web Ads

New visitors make their initial decision about a website in less than three seconds, so your ad copy must be clear, relevant, and eye-catching. This chapter walks you through the rules for writing online ads that convey your brand and convert clicks into sales, traffic, and signups. You'll learn how to understand your product, understand your audience, and then connect the two clearly and precisely.

- Write ads that satisfy a need and create a lasting impression.

- Craft copy for websites, email, direct mail, and social media.

- Know when to use formal or conversational language.

- Lay out an ad in an F or Z pattern.

- Use SEO keywords to gain the attention of search engines.

- Develop a tone and persona that addresses your specific audience.

- Hit your revenue, awareness, acquisition, and retention goals.

- Invoke psychological triggers such as priming, social proof, and price constructs.

- Overcome loss aversion in potential customers.

- Use online tools to define and measure metrics for each ad campaign.

- Avoid pitfalls like passive voice, weak headlines, marketese, and jargon.

- Include a call to action to close the deal.

Guidelines for Web Ads

The F-Pattern vs. the Z-Pattern

Effective online ad and sales copy tells a story or describes your offering over the course of a section or a page. The first rule of online advertising is:

> *Don't design your online ad campaigns in the same way that you design your print ads.*

The web isn't print. Online ad copy requires a clear message and an easily understandable progression. Clever online ads that make the

The F-pattern

reader work won't do as well as those that are simple and easy to follow. A full-page newspaper ad might look beautiful and impress someone at a cafe, but a webpage that has only a few words and branding will likely leave a reader wondering, "Okay, now what?"

Though online readers and print readers usually have different expectations, their eyes tend to behave the same. Eyetracking studies show that most people read webpages in an F-shaped pattern. This pattern mimics how you read a book: start at the top, then read right, go down a line, then read right, and so on, with a decreasing attention rate as you progress down the page.

An ad layout that uses an F-pattern typically contains left-aligned headlines, followed by left-aligned value-proposition points, followed by a left-aligned call to action (page 28). Because the F-pattern is familiar, readers don't need to be trained how to read your copy—they can quickly read it as if it were a novel. Unfortunately, since most readers *can* read it quickly, they *do* read it quickly, probably quicker than you'd like. Several studies have shown that less than fifty percent of users scroll beyond the first few paragraphs.

The Z-pattern

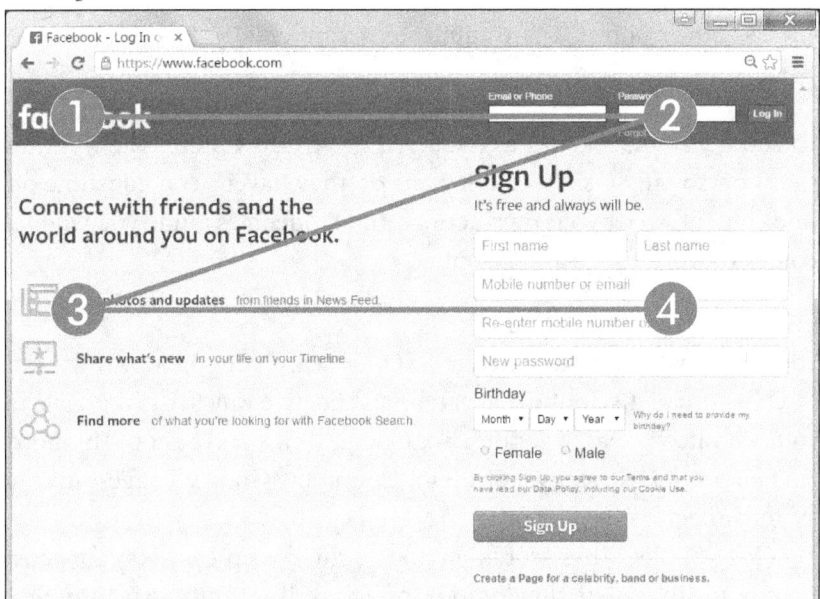

The Z-pattern tends to hold a reader's attention longer than the F-pattern. To create a Z-shaped pattern, superimpose a large letter Z on the page. Place the items that you want the reader to see first along the top edge of the Z. The eye will naturally follow the path of the Z, so your goal is to place the call to action (page 28) at the bottom right. Along the path of the Z, include bits of information that build to the call to action.

Which layout should you use for your ad copy? If you feel that a reader will make a purchase by remembering only one key piece of your value proposition (one feature or one benefit), then use the Z-pattern to force the reader's focus. On the other hand, if you're telling a story that builds your case over one or more paragraphs, then use the F-pattern.

In 1997, Jakob Nielsen of the Nielsen Norman Group published a landmark study titled "How Users Read on the Web" (*nngroup.com/articles/how-users-read-on-the-web*). This study determined that online content that was concise, scannable, and objective was 124% more readable than promotional "marketese" writing found on many commercial websites. So, as a copywriter:

- Use as few words as possible (concise)

- Use bullet points where applicable (scannable)

- Remove bias (objective)

Take a step back and ask yourself, "Why do I prefer the websites that I personally visit? What layouts do they have?" You consume online content, so let your own actions and tendencies guide you when it comes to word usage and layout.

Content Freshness and SEO

You've probably heard the term SEO, or search engine optimization. SEO is a broad discipline that can be an effective way to draw people to your website via search engines like Google, Bing, and Yahoo. This book isn't about SEO strategy, but I'll touch on how Google's page-ranking system affects your content.

Google, like other search engines, provides an easy way for most people to find what they're looking for online. But even though a particular Google search might return thousands or millions of results, most people don't look beyond the first page of search results—or even beyond the top three results on the first page, according to some surveys. So ranking as high as possible for a given set of search keywords is crucial.

Google is secretive about their search algorithms, but they do publish public guidelines for improving a page's rank, and other details can be gleaned from Google's patent applications. One of the most important criteria for ranking a document is its "freshness." In general, the value assigned to a page tends to decrease as its content ages. So, other things being equal, new content is more valuable than old. In ad copy, however, there's a tendency to set it and forget it. But you should strive to examine your on-page content regularly (every ninety days or more frequently). If there's something new and relevant that can be published, then do so. But don't force it. Google's web-crawling spiders (internet robots) severely penalize content that doesn't directly apply to a search. As do most visitors. Here are a few options for freshening content:

- **Seasonal changes**. Is there a seasonal aspect to your content? Do you sell your product or service differently in the winter than in the summer?

- **Technological developments**. Have there been any technological developments or product releases that affect your own product? If you offer an app that works on all Apple devices, for example, then update your content to show how your app works on the latest iPhone or Apple Watch.

When you create a new page or update an existing one, always leave your older content live to capitalize on valuable incoming links. These links are indexed by Google's search algorithms and lead to consistently higher rankings in search results.

Language and Branding

In the past decade or so, the language found in many types of ads has moved away from the professional and toward the casual. It's the responsibility of the speaker, not the listener, to make sure that the listener understands what's being conveyed. When you craft ad copy, your mission is to:

- **Convey the value proposition concisely and objectively.** If you're selling iPad training courses to people over the age of fifty, then you'll probably want to use proper sentence casing and use as little slang and jargon as possible. If you're selling to Millennials, then you might want to use ad copy that's more conversational and cute than professional.

- **Consider your audience.** If a father is buying life insurance to protect his entire family, then, regardless of his age and background, he expects to see professional language on an ad that reads like it was written by a lawyer, not a teenager.

- **Pay attention to what you're selling.** The company Carbonmade.com, for example, helps people create and manage online portfolios of illustrations, photographs, and other creative works. They appeal to a young, hip demographic, so their on-page content skews to convey a non-serious impression.

- **Be authentic.** People quickly form impressions of what a company embodies, so straying too far from authenticity can be disastrous. Think of how many traditional companies have tried to seem hip on social media only to come across as fake.

- **Consider how ad copy affects SEO.** The words that you write can impact your company's search engine optimization efforts. If you work for a small company, then using consistent terminology can actually help your ranking. For larger enterprises, going off-message can hurt branding.

- **Use or create a brand language guide.** If your company has a branding style guide for graphic design, then add the use of brand language to it. Knowing what terms to use, when to use them, and how to speak directly to your target audience are important parts of being an advertising professional. If you work for a smaller organization, then create a brand language guide that describes what your organization needs to craft a consistent message. These guidelines will also help employees amplify the company's message with a consistent tone and voice.

Goals of Web Ads

Revenue vs. Awareness Goals

Before you type a single word on your keyboard, ask yourself, "What exactly do I hope to achieve with this ad?" The advertising world is full of ads that have gone viral, but ultimately didn't make a cent for the company that created them. Likewise, plenty of companies have created ads that only led to "Okay, now what?" moments for readers—they read the entire ad and then saw a call to action that either made no sense or was too aggressive.

Most companies assume that sales equals success. But what about an ad that raises the awareness of your brand? Can you measure the exact revenue derived from this type of campaign? Perhaps, but by setting awareness goals for your ads in addition to revenue goals, you can understand what factors might eventually lead to more revenue in the future as well as the present.

Revenue goals (or revenue-driving goals) are those goals that have been identified as leading directly to revenue. If you sell shoes, then the revenue goal is shoe sales. An ad might talk about how great the shoes are, and then end with a Buy Now button. A revenue goal can also be the next step in a longer sales process. Software as a Service (SaaS) firms, for example, often offer a link to request a demonstration or contact a salesperson.

What if sales isn't your primary objective? Most companies also tend to focus on awareness goals (or interest goals) even if they don't realize it. That same shoe ad may choose to forgo the Buy Now button in lieu of a field where readers can type their email address to get free coupons. Or the ad might have a Find Your Nearest Location button. While neither of these actions leads directly to an increase in revenue, they do increase awareness, which might eventually lead to revenue.

A revenue goal's advantage is clear: money. Its main disadvantage is its lower intention and conversion rates. It's often hard to make a significant dent in sales. Only about 10% of online shoppers actually take action by adding items to their online shopping cart (low intention); of that 10%, almost 80% leave before completing the purchase (low conversion). Conversely, the main disadvantage of an awareness goal is that it doesn't put money in your pocket (immediately). Its advantage is its ability to retain customer interest as a direct result of a less-painful call to action (page 28).

If you create an ad that's effective at driving shoe sales (a revenue goal), then more customers will click the Buy Now button and purchase your shoes. But if you add an awareness goal to the mix, then you can find out what customers respond to and then ask them for a less-painful action to keep them exposed to further marketing material:

Revenue goals + Awareness goals = Effective ads

Get people to click an ad, and they'll buy your product and then go about their day. Get people to sign up for your emails, and they'll see every ad that you create, potentially leading to a much higher revenue per customer.

Acquisition Goals

Advertising to a new customer is similar to speed dating, but even faster. From the moment that a customer sees your ad to the moment they decide to proceed or pass, they're making constant value judgments about the ad and ad copy.

If someone is a new customer, then you're looking to acquire their business (an acquisition goal). The entire discipline of consumer choice theory and consumer marketing is devoted to acquiring customers. I'll summarize a few of their main concepts with respect to ad copy:

- **Start with your value proposition.** Put your best foot forward by starting with your value proposition, which is the thing that you have that customers want and competitors can't offer. Defining a value proposition is a difficult and time-consuming task, but it's crucial to get right. The value proposition of the Apple iPad, for example, might be a list of stories outlining its many different personal and commercial uses.

- **Focus on what the customer wants.** What about a product in a competitive and largely undifferentiated market, such as auto insurance? The insurance company GEICO created the value proposition "15 minutes can save you 15% or more on your car insurance" to trump what their competitors offer and focus on what customers want (to save money). GEICO's value proposition is quite specific—they didn't just say, "We'll save you money."

After the value proposition is properly identified and inserted in your ad, the rest of your ad should make that value proposition clear, understandable, and attainable: VigorAde is the first energy drink to offer this unique blend of electrolytes. It's only $2, which is much cheaper than competing energy drinks. And it can be yours now by simply visiting your local grocery store.

The value proposition should answer the who, what, and why questions that customers ask themselves (consciously or subconsciously) when they first encounter an ad for your product or service as new readers. A proper value proposition answers these three reader questions immediately:

- Who are you?

- What are you offering me?

- Why should I care?

What about the little voice that people hear in the back of their heads when they're reading an ad? Loss aversion (page 21) refers to the tendency for people to strongly prefer avoiding losses than acquiring gains. In other words, people are more afraid to make the wrong decision than they are excited to make the right decision—they don't want to be taken advantage of.

If you're viewing an ad from a company that has a long and established history, like Apple or Toyota, then that voice tends to be relatively quiet. But if you're looking to buy a Rolex from OmarsAwesomeWatchChalet.com, then that voice can be a deafening roar. Always answer the voice of doubt that every customer hears. Include some sort of anti-anxiety or trust message in your ad for readers who are unfamiliar with your company. Put yourself in the customer's shoes and answer the who, what, and why questions.

Retention Goals

You wouldn't talk to a new customer in the same way that you would talk to a longtime customer, and neither should your advertising. Here's a tip from Sarah Cox, an advertising copywriter in Chicago:

I once worked at a company that operated purely on a retention-marketing basis. They had reached their limit and simply couldn't support bringing in new customers. Every ad that I wrote for them was for returning customers only. No new ones came through the door. Here's the most important thing that I learned: in an acquisition ad, focus on who, what, and why; in a retention ad, first acknowledge the relationship and then present a custom offer. What you're trying to sell them isn't as important as why it's relevant for them specifically.

Simply acknowledging that you have a relationship with a customer instantly increases the sense of relevance that the customer feels. But generating that feeling is hard to do. When that feeling takes hold, the customer's mindset changes from "this company is talking to everybody" to "this company is talking to me." For this reason, retention marketing tends to have a conversational writing style and air of familiarity, as if you're chatting with a customer. You can do so by mentioning a previous purchase or account activity, using their name in the introduction, or customizing the offer to exclude new customers. Here's an example of an effective retention-based ad:

Hi John,
Congratulations on your new mountain bike! In appreciation for doing business with us, buy a bike helmet today and save 25%.

This ad acknowledges a specific customer (John) and his purchasing history (mountain bike). It also presents a customized purchase recommendation (bike helmet), an incentive to act (save 25%) for a limited time (today), and John's status as a returning customer (in appreciation). If an ad doesn't offer a deal that's related to a customer's prior purchase, then at least acknowledge the existing relationship:

> Hi John,
> Because you're a returning customer, we'd like to offer you a discount on your next purchase ...

Customer retention isn't only about getting more from returning customers; it's also about reducing the churn or loss of your client base. While advertising usually won't be the tool that you'll use to reduce loss, there's the danger that over-advertising to your existing customer database will scare them off. Offers need to be worthwhile. Make sure that the offer you're presenting is actually something that customers might take you up on.

Ad copy can be an effective tool in creating a long-lasting relationship with your customers, but it must be done right. Talking to customers in a conversational and familiar way disarms them, so they're more receptive to your ads. Acknowledge your relationship and then give them a relevant offer. Let them know that you're not just speaking to anybody, you're speaking to them specifically. People like to be remembered and your ad copy should reflect that.

Ads for Different Media Types

Website Ads

Ignore all the stories about how the modern attention span has shrunk to that of a goldfish (eight seconds). Online customers will give you as much time as *they* need to decide on what you're advertising. Eight seconds? Two seconds? A minute? Who knows—no two people are alike. If your ad creates positive value in the mind of a prospect, then that person will give you ample time. When you're creating your online ad copy, don't think about an eight-second countdown. Instead, say it fast and say it properly:

- Remove all marketing fluff and distractions

- Get to the point quickly

- Present the offer and benefits clearly

- Reduce your word count

Readers don't care about your amazing writing style, how great your company is, why you're different, and why the competition stinks. They want to know what value you can provide to them, and they want it in the first two or three sentences. The modern online consumer is savvy enough to see through bold headlines, autoplay videos, and other gimmicks. In fact, introducing your ad forcibly can backfire—when's the last time that you reacted positively to a popup message?

A primary consideration is to ensure that your copy works with the ad design. Eyetracking studies show that most people read online content as they would read a written book, yet many designers create jarring webpages that use ample whitespace to make the reader focus on certain content.

A key benefit of online writing is that you can easily track how your words are laid out and presented through the use of A/B testing (*wikipedia.org/wiki/A/B_testing*), eyetracking tools, heat maps, and click maps. You can measure ad effectiveness by using analytics and feedback tools like Hotjar.com and Clicktale.com. In conjunction with your graphic design team, vary the spacing and layout and track the ad's effectiveness with each permutation.

Email Ads

You've just spent hours writing and editing a perfect email with an irresistible subject line. It's going to be a hit with your audience because you're selling them a service that could actually help them in their daily life. You hit Send and away it goes. It arrives in the recipient's inbox—and is deleted immediately, unread. Here are a few tips to help you avoid that fate:

- **Make your email responsive on all devices**. People check their emails on laptops, desktops, phones, and tablets, while at work, at home, on a train, standing in line, and doing their laundry. Plan how your email will look on a mobile device first, then add sales copy and elements as needed for full-screen (desktop) resolution. Strive for simple eyeflow: every sales-based email should contain only one column. The information hierarchy should be one or two short paragraphs that lead to a large, eye-catching call to action (page 28). People browse with their thumbs on mobile, so make sure that the call to action is positioned in a place that thumbs can reach, and that it's large enough to click or tap easily.

- **Keep copy to a minimum.** When people see text-heavy emails, they think it's going to be an account update or a similarly dry message, so keep your copy to an absolute minimum. Here's what to write in your email:

  - A headline that addresses a potential problem.
  - A subhead or short first paragraph that talks about how you can solve the problem.
  - One short paragraph with important information.
  - A call to action.

Nothing more. It's easy to delete an email, and most people don't really want to read an email, so always strive for a small word count.

- **Customize the subject line.** Make your subject line weird. Most people have such a strong feeling of inbox malaise that it's hard for your one message to stick out. The more original and relevant your subject line is, the higher the likelihood that the recipient will open your message. Use emojis. Include the recipient's first name. Offer a tip to solve a problem. Never play it safe in the subject line. Recipients probably won't open "Special offer for you" or "Check out our newest product." But they probably will open "How can a pair of pants make your life better?"

- **Include a friendly call to action.** Don't ask for much. Email is a low-involvement communications medium, and because you're going to take the recipient elsewhere after they click, you must first reassure them that they're not going to go somewhere scary. So instead of telling them to "Buy Now" or "Join Now," keep it light and say "Check It Out" or "Take a Tour." Think of it this way: if you just met someone and wanted to sell them something in the first thirty seconds, then what would be your action statement?

- **Write in a conversational style.** Avoid big words and jargon when simple, common speech terms work. Instead of saying, "This service revolutionizes business," say, "We've got a better way of doing that exact same thing you're doing."

- **Try new things with email.** Email marketing entails low costs and low risks. With the right strategy, it can be a big money-maker. The next time that someone tells you email is dead or that email is a bad way to drive action, ask them whether they've opened an email today. Or yesterday. Chances are they'll tell you, "I did."

Direct Mail Ads

Paper. Printing. Sorting. Packaging. Shipping. Postage. Receiving. Response tracking. Old-school direct mail advertising is complicated, expensive, and time-consuming, but it has one huge advantage over all online ads: tangibility. When you receive an email or look at a webpage, you're reading code on a device. But when you receive something in your mailbox, you can actually hold it, turn it, open it, and use it. Paper engages your tactile senses in a way that dots on a screen never will. And when you're engaged with a direct mail piece, no other browser tabs are competing for your attention. Direct mail captures your attention by giving you something to grasp. To capitalize on this advantage, write ad copy that's:

- **Informative.** Tell readers about a new product, why your company is special, who you are, what you do, and so on. If you're selling a food product, then list the ingredients and nutritional information. Always explain how your product solves a problem. And don't worry about length—this isn't Twitter.

- **Useful.** Your goal for direct mail advertising is to create a piece that lasts. You want someone to read it, use it, and then toss it on their coffee table to return to later. So create something that's useful. If you're selling a sports drink, then include a printout of healthy drink recipes for after a workout. That's something people can put on their fridge and use over and over again.

- **Branded**. Usefulness creates a favorable branding impression for the recipient. The next time that customer is trying to choose between Brand A and Brand B sports drink, they'll remember your brand from that thing they have on their fridge, and you might have a customer for life. Direct mail may be a bigger branding force than any other medium.

- **Delightful**. Create an incentive for reading your direct mail piece. If someone has read your four-paragraph ad for delicious cookies, then why not end the piece with a coupon for a free box of cookies? Make it worth their while, and they'll be hooked. When you send another direct mail piece, yours will be the first envelope that they open. I've been part of campaigns where recipients have called the company to make sure we had their right address so they didn't miss out on another piece.

Social Media Ads

It seems like everyone nowadays is checking their feed or updating their status on social networks. Thousands of these networks exist across the world, but I'm going to talk about only the two biggest platforms for social media ads: Twitter and Facebook. Although they're very different networks, ads on both involve the same four components:

A Facebook ad

- An image
- A headline
- A post title
- A description

Here are some tips for writing social media ads:

- **Use related components.** Make sure that all four ad components work in unity. Your image should reflect the title, and the description should impart the value implicit in the headline. Saying one thing and then linking to somewhere unexpected is a big mistake. Examine each of the four components of your ad to make sure that they all tell the same story. If not, then don't post the ad.

- **Remember your place.** A Facebook timeline is a very personal place to advertise. Your audience is scrolling down their timeline, looking at pictures of their friends and family, and then here you come trying to sell something. A good Facebook ad is chameleon-like, sticking out just enough to avoid close detection. To do this, use an image that features people. Because most pictures on a Facebook feed are of people, such images create a consistent flow that isn't too jarring. Don't scream about a special limited-time offer. Mention your product in a conversational manner, as if a friend was posting about it. A friend wouldn't post "Get your free whitepaper about winning business tactics." A bit better is "Are you running a triathlon? Maybe this can help." On Twitter, which has a 140-character limit, be careful not to write in shorthand. Don't change your brand's tone for Twitter. Writing "ppl" instead of "people" may save characters, but it will decrease your brand value on Twitter. Stay true to your brand—don't use shorthand just because that's how other people are tweeting.

- **Pay attention to feedback.** Every post can generate feedback. You post your ad, and replies come rolling in a minute later. Some are positive. Some are negative. In response, engage customers in such a way to build brand evangelists, always staying on tone and on brand.

Psychological Triggers

The Psychology of Ads

The relatively new field of marketing psychology seeks to give marketers insights into:

- How people make purchasing decisions

- How people differentiate between competing products

- How much information purchasers actually need before they commit

Psychology plays a strong role in marketing strategy. For example, are you more likely to buy food when you're full or hungry? Recall the last time that you went to Ikea. The ad for cheap food appeared about three-quarters of the way through the store, when you had expended enough energy walking and browsing to be hungry and in need of a small psychological push to finish your trip through the store.

Consumer behavior is a wide-ranging discipline that seeks to understand everything from the mindset of early tech adopters to how items on a shelf can best be positioned for maximum exposure. For decades, countless marketing studies have helped explain what people are thinking when they read an ad. What's the best font size? At what point do people lose interest in what you're selling? Controlled studies, of varying degrees of ethicality, have sought to answer thousands of questions like these.

Every successful company has at some point used psychological marketing concepts in their ad copy. If you're not trying to understand how people think and act, then you're just hoping that your ads will work because you're such an awesome writer. The rest of this chapter discusses some psychological triggers that you can use in your copy to help influence a reader's decision-making process.

Priming

Even people who are unfamiliar with marketing psychology have probably heard of priming. In a nutshell, priming uses a stimulus to affect a later stimulus. Think of priming as planting a seed for later action. In a well-known priming experiment, psychologists found that people were faster to recognize words when similar or related words were given first. For example, subjects who saw the word "nurse" recognized the word "doctor" faster than an unrelated term, like "bread."

You don't have to be a cognitive scientist to see that priming makes sense. It taps into our memories and sensory perception, and allows our brain to group things. For ad copy, you can use priming to your advantage in two ways:

- **Stimulus priming**. Use a condition or situation to prime readers. Suppose that you're selling sunscreen. If people are reading your ad in the Pacific Northwest during winter, when it's rainy every day, then it probably won't appeal to them. But what if you use a sunny beach as a background image and introduce your ad with "Right now in Maui, Sarah is getting burned."

Just mentioning a sunny place primes the reader to receive your message. The use of a sunny image and the word "Maui" helps readers picture a situation in which they would be Sarah and need sunscreen.

- **Homophone priming**. Use sound-alike words (homophones) to prime readers. Homophone priming is related to stimulus priming, but uses the sound of words to prepare the reader for action. In the sunscreen example, if the call to action (page 28) is "Buy now," then you can use homophone priming earlier in the ad by using a phrase like "Bye, bye, rainy days." "Bye" sounds the same as "buy," so you're influencing readers without them necessarily realizing it.

The key to priming is to think of both the initial stimulus and the ultimate action stimulus. Does priming always work? No—it's a gentle suggestion, not a forceful push. And overusing it disrupts the flow of ad copy.

Social Proof

While everyone has their own wants and needs, in most situations people tend to act in the same or similar way. The power of conformity can pay off for ad copywriters when it comes time for readers to make a purchase decision. By mentioning that other people have conformed to, or purchased, what you're offering, you're tapping into the herd mentality. People place greater trust in something that they see or hear other people have done. Social proof must be:

- **Believable**. How many times have you driven by McDonald's and seen a sign similar to "Billions of burgers served"? That's impressive, but what if that sign said "Over 14 burgers sold"? You can apply this technique to your own ads, but don't just make up a large number. You're going to make a lot of people skeptical if you write "Over 5 billion scarves sold." You can round up or project a bit, but social proof in ad copy works only if it's honest and believable. If you have low sales or customer numbers, then you probably shouldn't use social proof in an ad. If not many people have taken advantage of what you're offering, then that could cause readers to ask, "Why not?"

- **Relevant**. You want readers to think, "That's a lot of people just like me." If you're running an ad in AARP magazine, then write "Over 50,000 retired people trust the heart medicine." Experiment with the granularity of social proof. If you're marketing in the United States, then the phrase "Over one million Americans" is going to be much more effective than "Over one million customers." But a more-targeted phrase like "Over one million Californians" usually performs worse than "Over one million Americans." Why? Perhaps people identify as Americans first and Californians second. Or maybe people want relevance, but not too much relevance.

- **Stress-reducing**. Use social proof to reduce anxiety or doubt in a potential customer. If all the reader has to do to get 10% off is click a button to get a discount code, then the level of risk is low for the reader. If the reader has to hand over their name, address, phone number, and other personal information to get a free book, then that's a bit risky. To garner some trust, add a bit of social proof like "Over 25,000 people have already signed up."

Used correctly, social proof can be one of the most effective tools in an ad campaign. Whether you lead with it or whether it's a minor call-out should be related directly to the level of risk that the reader is going to feel. Test different numbers and granularities, and let the data tell you what works best with your audience.

Price

Thousands of marketing experiments that involve pricing show that changing the way that a price is presented in an ad matters, and many times is the difference between a new customer and a lost sale. As an ad copywriter, you might be thinking, "I don't set the price of the thing. I just sell it." But that's not entirely true. You can offer a chair for "$100 plus free shipping" or "$90 plus $10 shipping." It's still the same $100 chair, but the potential buyer sees two entirely different price constructs.

Perhaps you don't have that much leeway in your company. If you can't change how a price is presented, then you can use other techniques to manipulate how the price is perceived. Price is a relative concept. Here are a few tactics for making a price seem lower in an ad:

- **Divided cost**. In a study, researcher John Gourville discovered that simply mentioning the divided time of a price results in a lower overall perception of that price, without leaving out the actual price. To apply this finding in ads, introduce a lower divided price of what you're offering. In the $100 chair example above, start your ad description with "For just $3 a day you can relax in your favorite new chair." The price hasn't changed, but you've made the $100 less formidable.

- **Time benefit**. No matter the price of your product or service, it's going to be too much money for some customers. People associate price with pain. But if the joy or utility is equal to or greater than the pain, then potential buyers are more likely to make a purchase. To shift the conversation in your ad away from the pain, focus on how the product or service relates to time. Researchers Cassie Mogilner and Jennifer Aaker theorize that time increases focus on product experience. To apply this finding in ads, focus on the benefits of time spent with the product rather than its monetary investment (affordability). In the $100 chair example above, write "Think of how comfortable you'll be all day," rather than "Our chair is budget friendly." That sounds like a distraction because it is. If you can distract readers from the price, yet still have them register the price, then you're off to a good start.

- **Higher price mention**. Introduce a larger number before the price. Yes, this counter-intuitive tactic actually works. In two separate studies, researchers found that simply exposing subjects to a higher number at some point before the price led subjects to perceive that price as smaller. To apply this finding in ads, put a number larger than the price earlier in the ad. If you're selling a $2 pack of pencils, then write "Pack of 6 pencils for $2" rather than "Pack of pencils for $2."

These three tactics—divided cost, time benefit, and higher price mention—might apply to your next project, but if not there are countless others. No matter what tactics you use, be sure to address the presentation of the price and how it relates to the reader's perception of pain.

Loss Aversion

Which experience would you rather have: finding free money or not losing money? Study after study has shown that loss aversion is real. In general, people prefer to avoid losses rather than acquire gains. In other words, losing money is more painful than gaining money is pleasurable. In marketing, this concept presents itself in several ways:

- **Fear of missing out**. Rational humans are worried that they'll be left out of group decisions. The thought that we might make the wrong decision and be excluded from the group is a strong evolutionary trait that can be seen in ads everywhere. Some ads even say "Don't be left out." This approach works but it's a fairly negative way to create an ad.

- **Endowment effect**. People place a higher value on an item simply because they already own it. If the generic coffee mug in your cupboard cost you $3.00, then you, as a rational actor, would sell that mug to someone for more than $3.00. Whatever your price, you would want more than its original value because it's *your* mug. Proper presentation maximizes the endowment effect. In an ad, present the product as something that the customer *already* owns—they just need to take an action and you'll release it to them. When you buy movie tickets or airplane tickets online, you'll always see a message saying they will hold *your* tickets for the next two minutes or so. The tickets are already "yours" even though you haven't paid for them.

Loss aversion taps into the deep insecurities, but tactics like the endowment effect can help you overcome them. To figure out how you can best use the endowment effect, put yourself in the mind of customers who are on the fence about buying your product. What are they scared of? Your ad should always address a problem, whether that problem is related to their financial life, working life, or personal life. Turn that pain into pleasure, and your ad will have a chance of resonating with your target audience.

Personas and Tone

Customer Personas

One of the biggest issues that companies face in their ad campaigns is how to talk to their audience. If you have a specific type of potential buyer, then you can use personas to talk to them on their terms. Defining personas entails investigating a group and then boiling them down to no more than two or three specific people who represent your audience. Let's look at three different scenarios:

- **Small business.** You work for a small business that has a small web presence. Your best data-gathering methods are those that private investigators use: watching and interviewing. If you work for a brick-and-mortar business, then spend a few hours observing who enters your store. Are they primarily male or female? Professional, casual, or blue collar? After they leave, ask the employees what type of questions these customers asked. Are there any overall trends or common themes? If you work for a mail-order or web-based business, then include a customer survey with each mailed purchase and tie it to a discount to increase the likelihood that the customer completes and returns it.

- **Medium company.** You work for a medium-size company that has a moderate web presence. You can use website survey tools like Qualaroo.com and Clicktale.com, along with email survey tools like SurveyMonkey.com, to ask pointed, direct, or broad questions that can help you define your ad copy strategy. Often you'll uncover hidden gems in terms of what your customers are looking for.

- **Large company.** You work for a large company that has a large web presence. Believe it or not, the larger your company, the harder it can be to learn more about your customers. If your firm doesn't have a dedicated data team, then you might get significant push-back and challenges when you want to contact customers directly or put a survey up on your website. For companies like these, your best approach might be to use social media to get instant feedback to your questions.

The amount of information that defines a persona varies by company. Some companies go as far as trying to learn what flavors of ice cream their customers prefer, but that's probably overkill. In most cases, you need to know only the problems of your customers and how your product or service can make their lives better.

After you've fleshed out the personas, write ad copy as if you were talking to a specific persona. You're doing them a favor. You know what their problems are and you know that your product can help. How would you tell them that if they were sitting at the same table as you? You wouldn't use marketing-speak. You'd start by acknowledging their pain, and then tell them how your product can help.

Suppose that your product is VigorAde, a sports drink. The target persona, call her Olivia, is training for a triathlon and is worried that she won't finish the event. She has two kids and a full-time job. Luckily for her, you have a sports drink that can help her achieve her goal of completing a triathlon. Olivia obviously doesn't care that VigorAde comes in various neon colors. Your ad for her would revolve around how VigorAde will help her achieve her fitness goals. "Trusted by more triathletes than any other sports drink." You're speaking directly to Olivia and her needs, instead of throwing ideas at the wall.

Tone

How do personas talk about your product or service? Do they use inflated adjectives like "amazing," or restrained adjectives like "efficient"? Tone is important because it sets your brand apart. Most ads look the same and say the same thing. When you think of an ad for a software company, you probably picture stock photos, labeled diagrams, and intimidating jargon. A counterexample is Slack.com, a team-collaboration service that uses straightforward, conversational language such as "Slack is free to use for as long as you want for teams of all sizes."

Big results follow from using an original, conversational tone that resonates with your audience. The point of every ad is to create an emotional response. Most purchasing decisions are Type 1 decisions, meaning their origin resonates with the emotional area of the brain. Your goal is to get people to like your brand and product and feel something emotional. Think back to two classic TV commercials: Coca-Cola's "Mean Joe Greene" (*youtube.com/watch?v=xffOCZYX6F8*) and Apple's "1984" (*youtube.com/watch?v=2zfqw8nhUwA*). They were arresting ads that made viewers feel something. Nostalgia, in the case of Coca-Cola, and amazement, in the case of Apple. It's no surprise that these two brands still use those tones in their ad campaigns.

Tone should be a direct reflection of your audience. The tone of an ad for a funeral home will differ from that of a muffler repair shop. Tone also needs to be authentic and unforced. The public perception of some brands is set in stone. A FedEx ad campaign isn't going to feature a skateboarding tortoise who talks like a teenage girl. Stay the course. Only a few companies—Old Spice, for example—have ever been able to remake their image completely.

Use restraint with regard to tonal changes. If you're writing a product description, then keep it technical, but maybe add some personality into the headline or introduction. Always make any changes to the tone gradually. Ads that try too hard just come across as sad. As in dating, play it cool, but not too cool. And always have an effective call to action (page 28).

There's no universally preferred tone. If your ads are primarily online, then test different approaches and themes in your ad campaigns via A/B testing (*wikipedia.org/wiki/A/B_testing*) tools like Optimizely.com or VWO.com, which let you tweak, optimize, and personalize your website.

Readers should be able to find your ads via search engines. Search engines such as Google, Bing, and Yahoo scour the web for keywords, index them, and present them in search results to readers. Think carefully about which keywords or key phrases you put in your ads, and even where you place them within the headline.

Keep in mind that while readers may appreciate wit and style, search engine algorithms certainly do not. If copywriting is considered to be both an art and a science, then keyword choice and placement is the science part. SEO (search engine optimization) is the process of affecting the visibility of a website or a webpage in a search engine's unpaid results. Two of the best SEO tools for researching keywords are Google Keyword Planner (*ads.google.com/home/tools/keyword-planner*), to get keyword ideas and statistics, and Google Trends (*trends.google.com*), to see what's being searched for around the world.

Another way to come up with keywords is to think like a searcher. If you were a reader and wanted to find a product like the one you're trying to sell, what words would you type into Google to locate it? You wouldn't type a pun or grandiloquent adjectives. You'd type the phrase at the heart of the need or problem. Those are your keywords.

After you decide on your keywords or key phrases, include them in your copy so that search engines will find them and present your ad to readers.

By using a tone that's reflective, authentic, and restrained, you can communicate with your potential customers as they like to be talked to. And possibly create lasting emotions that will keep them coming back to your ads.

Ad Dos and Don'ts

Use the Active Voice

Use active voice rather than passive voice in ads. In passive voice, the doer, also known as the subject, *receives* the action. In active voice, the subject has the agent role as the cause or initiator of the action. For example, the following sentence is in passive voice:

> VigorAde was developed by industry experts, and can change your daily routine.

In contrast, the following sentence is in active voice:

> Expertly developed VigorAde will change your life.

Passive voice makes thoughts, especially complex ones, hard to follow—the reader wonders who is doing what. A headline, for example, must grab the reader's attention immediately. If you use passive voice, then you increase the reader's cognitive load. Readers will spend more time thinking about what you mean rather than acting on what you're selling. The following passive-voice sentence leaves the reader wondering, "Does VigorAde change my life? Or is my life changed because I'm using it?"

> Your life will be changed by drinking VigorAde every day.

The active-voice version is clearer:

> Drinking VigorAde every day changes your life.

To make matters worse, passive ad copy tends to run longer than active ad copy, adding unnecessary words to your ad. In the two examples above, the passive version runs ten words and the active version runs seven words. In a medium like Twitter, which has a hard limit of 140 characters, using passive voice can actually hurt your ability to advertise.

Finally, passive voice is often a poor design choice. Readers who scan ads—that is, prospects who rarely read beyond the first few words—won't see the actual thing being offered or sold. In the following passive-voice sentence, just the initial words "Your life will be" are long and dull enough to lose the reader's interest immediately:

Your life will be changed by drinking VigorAde every day.

In the active-voice version, the words are clear and make a strong impression:

Drinking VigorAde every day changes your life.

In general, emphasize the call to action (page 28). Create a straight line to the conversion by using the active tone throughout your ad copy. The difference between passive and active voice can be subtle, but it can mean the difference between a confused reader and a motivated customer.

Write Effective Headlines

On the average, five times as many people read the headline as read the body copy. When you have written your headline, you have spent eighty cents out of your dollar.

–David Ogilvy

A headline (Chapter 2) is the first thing that your reader will read, so it's your only chance to make a great first impression. Effective headlines feature these four traits:

- **Grabs the reader's attention and then lets it go.** Use creative and imaginative ways to introduce the ad. Use conversational terms and avoid clichés and hucksterism. Instead of "Get This Limited-Time Offer on All Items in Stock," write, "Yes, We Have That Awesome Item You're Looking for at a Great Price." Your headline should segue naturally into the copy below, with no jarring change in tone (page 24).

- **Meets the customer's entry expectation.** Readers will often arrive at your ad via a search engine or a related prior webpage or email. When possible, reflect the entry keywords or terms in your headline.

- **Addresses a problem.** The point of an ad is to sell something. The first thing that the reader thinks is, "Will this product make my life better in any way?" Understanding the motivations and needs of your customers is especially crucial in headline writing. If you sell brooms that also polish hardwood floors, then you can market to janitorial services by using a headline like "Save Time and Energy Cleaning Hardwood Floors."

- **Makes sense**. Use simple, clear language. A headline isn't the place to persuade someone; it's the place to clarify what you're selling.

Don't spend hours trying to write the perfect headline. Just write one that meets the four traits above and then move on. If you're agonizing over a headline, here are a few tips:

- **Write the headline last**. Normally, a headline is the first thing you'd write, but if you view your ad as a conversation with your customer, then knowing how the entire conversation went might help you figure out the best opening.

- **Swap the headline and subhead**. If your ad has a headline and a subheadline, then switch them. When ad copywriters write a headline and subhead, they tend to make the headline their big moment (to show how clever they are), and then return to Earth by connecting the subhead to the customer's needs in a way that flows to the main copy. The customer doesn't care how clever the copywriter is. Swapping the headline and subhead flips the focus from the writer to the reader.

The Call to Action (CTA)

A call to action (CTA) is the final instruction to the reader in your ad's sales funnel. A CTA is a button, text link, or graphic that takes the reader to a landing page when clicked. Most CTAs start with a verb. For example, a common CTA is a Join Now or Sign Up button that links a page to the account creation process.

You can view a CTA as the end of the argument that you're presenting. In every ad that you

Call to action Sign Up button

create, you're actually arguing why someone should buy your product, and your CTA should close that argument. If you win the argument, then the reader will want something. Clicking the CTA should fulfill that want:

- Buy Now
- Shop Now
- View Products
- Learn More
- Find Out More
- Talk to Us
- Sign Up
- Join
- Join Now
- Join Free
- Log In with [Google/Facebook/Twitter/LinkedIn]
- Get Started
- Let's Start
- Contact Us
- Book Now
- Download
- Download Now
- Free Download
- Download Your Ebook
- Subscribe
- Subscribe Today
- Let's Do It

- Get the Secret Now
- Reserve Your Spot Today
- Get Access Now
- Get it Free
- Get Your Free Sample
- Get Your Coupon Code
- Save 10%
- Save $150
- Unlimited Access for $99
- Play Free
- Go Premium
- Yes, Please
- Request a Demo
- Get More Info
- What We Do
- Try it Free
- Try it Now
- Get the Next Issue Free
- Give a Gift
- Claim Your Free Trial
- Attend Our Event
- Register Now
- Be Awesome
- Follow the Magic
- Check it Out

- Yes, Take Me There

- Put X to Work for You

- Show Me My X

- Build an X

- Send an X

- Get Free X

- Give X a Try

- Create My X

- I Want to X

- Discover X

- Sign Up to X

- View X

- Grab My X

Many CTAs contain the word "now" as a little push to get the reader to act immediately. Otherwise, an interested reader is more than likely to say, "I'll just save this for later,"—and then never return.

You can use the endowment effect (page 21) in a CTA. Recall that the endowment effect states that people place a higher value on an item simply because they already own it. To invoke this effect in an ad, pretend that the reader already has taken the action or already owns the product you're selling. All that they need to do is click the CTA for you to release it to them. Simply attributing ownership to what you're selling can be a slight motivational push. When you see the word "your" or "yours" in a CTA, the ad is usually making use of the endowment effect: Buy Your Tickets. Make It Yours. Upgrade Your Account. Order Yours Now.

It's not unusual for advertisers to become obsessed with improving their CTAs. In fact, CTAs may be the most common dependent variable in conversion optimization testing.

Content Marketing

With so much competition in the digital age, modern consumers expect to be rewarded for reading your advertisement. Traditional advertising isn't dead, but the transition to branded content consumption is proceeding full steam. Content marketing is targeted marketing material that's backed up by social media campaigns and is integrated with an overall acquisitions structure. Content marketing *isn't* a series of regular posts about a variety of topics, like you'd find on a blog.

Regardless of industry, companies that establish a content marketing strategy can leapfrog their more-stagnant competitors. If you sell plumbing tools, then connect customers to branded content about how to properly install pipes in a new construction. Not only are you talking about why your product exists, you're providing useful information.

Lots of tools are available to help you establish such a strategy quickly and painlessly. Content automation tools like Tumblr, ClearVoice, and Hootsuite make it easy to provide your customers with useful content. Google suggests presenting a large amount of content that's unique, specific, and of high quality. In other words, don't copy your competitors.

If there's one lesson to take away from this book, it's that advertising has to satisfy a need. Content marketing is really all about making your ad copy clear, relevant, and useful. Methods may have changed over the years, but creating effective copy for a traditional ad or a content marketing post still has the same function: inform the customer about your product and then tell them why it's relevant to them specifically.

2   Web Headlines

Knowing how to write candid and catchy headlines is the key to getting your message heard. Whether you write for blogs, websites, newsletters, press releases, or social media posts, you can learn how to craft attention-grabbing headlines with these essential techniques. In this chapter, you'll learn the art and science of writing killer headlines, with loads of examples along the way.

- Rise above the noise and capture the attention of readers.

- Preview a story, pull out the relevant benefits, and pack them into a headline.

- Give readers an exciting, accurate, and irresistible sense of a story.

- Know what to leave out of a headline.

- Engage readers with conflict, familiarity, or timeliness.

- Use vibrant language to set the tone for a story.

- Use correct punctuation and capitalization.

- Write subheads to describe a long or complex article.

- Use words and trends that engage readers.

- Learn the structural rules that keep a headline professional looking and grammatically sound.

- Use SEO keywords to gain the attention of search engines.

Summing Up a Story in a Few Words

To craft a headline that's both informative and intriguing, you must read the accompanying story closely to determine what it's really about, and then express that main idea in a few concise words. If someone else wrote the story and you're tasked with slapping a headline on it, then the challenging part is becoming familiar enough with the story to boil someone else's words—hundreds or even thousands of words—down to just a few that smartly sum up the rest. If you're writing a headline for your own story, then the task can be equally challenging, perhaps even more so. When you're that close to the material, it can be hard to step back far enough to get the big picture and whittle it down to a single predominant concept.

In either case, it helps to comb through the story carefully, looking for keywords (page 50) and ideas that you can pick out and put up on the marquee. If the story is well-written, then the information that you need will be near the top, typically in the first two or three paragraphs. Pinpoint the main "who" (who is the story about?) and the main "what" (what happened or what's the main action?). For example, the headline:

What's New for Photographers in the iPhone 11 Pro

indicates that the story's "who" is photographers and "what" is the new iPhone.

Another trick for conjuring a headline is to ask yourself how you would explain the story to a friend if you could do so in only six words (or five words or seven words). Try it. The challenge is to limit yourself. Creativity tends to flourish within strict boundaries.

Let's write a headline for a story about why it's advantageous for digital artists to learn some 3D skills. Let's start with:

Yes, You Need to Learn 3D

That's not bad. It gets the job done, but it's a bit dull. How about:

Yep—It's Time to Learn 3D

Blah. Not an attention-grabber.

You Need to Know 3D—Now

Too bossy.

> Ready to Learn 3D? Start Today.

Serviceable, but sounds too much like a sales pitch.

> Everyone Needs to Learn 3D. Ready?

This one works. It captures the article's tone, but it's a tad lifeless.

> Yes, as a Matter of Fact. You Do Need to Learn 3D.

That's better. This headline has just the right amount of personality.

As you can see, there are almost limitless possibilities for any given headline. If your headline is true to the story, then you're off to a good start.

You may be occasionally surprised to find that the article you end up with isn't the article that you (or the writer, if that's not you) set out to create. When that happens, don't fight it. Your job isn't to pay homage to the article that never was; it's to make sure that your headline reflects the final product and gets people to read it.

Grabbing the Reader's Attention

When was the last time that you stopped to read a story with a headline that was completely irrelevant to your life? Throughout this book, I'm going to give you lots of tips for making your headlines more engaging, appealing, and irresistible. But when it comes down to it, there's really only one reason that people stop to read a headline: they believe that there's something in it for them. It might be something that will help them solve a problem:

> How to Tell If You've Been Exposed to Lead

Or it might be something that will inform them about an issue they care about:

> Weekend Roadwork Expected to Cause Carmageddon

It might be to confirm or challenge an assumption they have:

> Why Hollywood Is Still Getting 3D Movies Wrong

Or teach them something valuable:

> Everything You Need to Know About Tomorrow's Solar Eclipse

Or get ahead at work:

> 15 Bad Habits That Could Cost You a Promotion

Or make them look smart or informed:

> NATO Enters the Migration Control Business

Potential readers always ask, "What's in it for me?" Your job as the headline writer is to figure out what that thing is and tap into it. Show your readers how a story is relevant to them and how it's going to benefit them directly. For example:

> How to Protect Your Garden from El Niño Storms

You can't be all things to all people, of course:

> How to El Niño-Proof Your Home No Matter Where You Live— Without Breaking the Bank

What you *can* do is take a hard look at your story and identify your ideal audience (that is, who stands to benefit most from it), and go after those people with a headline that makes clear how the article will benefit them by promising something of value.

Characteristics of Great Headlines

Headline enthusiasts are happy to tell you about their favorites. A New York Post story about a gunman who forced a woman to decapitate a tavern owner was headlined:

> Headless Body in Topless Bar

Here's a headline from the New York Daily News for a story about a travel agency that was selling bogus tours to Ireland:

> Tour Allure a Lie

But most headlines aren't so witty, horrific, unflinching, or precise. They need a little help to make them sparkle. The best headlines share the following four characteristics:

- **Unique**. Your headline won't stand out if it looks and sounds like most of the other headlines that your reader encounters in the course of a day. Think about what you can do to be a little different. Infuse your headline with personality. In the following headline, the word "actually" adds some unexpected attitude:

  Five Excel Tips You'll Actually Use

  Quirky phrasing makes this headline conversational:

  So, There's This New Yoga App ...

- **Useful**. Don't aim to merely amuse or distract the reader. Instead, define a purpose and fulfill a promise. Readers expect valuable, new information in return for the five minutes that it takes to read your article. If you can't promise your reader a useful read, then the headline writer on the next page will. Here's an example:

  Watch This Guy Hack Your Phone in Under Three Minutes

- **Specific**. Be direct and specific. The fastest way to lose a reader's respect and attention is to waste their time. The following three headlines for the same story range from broad to specific:

  A Possible Solution to Plastic Problem

  There's This Bacteria That Eats Plastic Bottles

  Could Plastic-Eating Bacteria Solve Our Trash Problems?

  The most specific headline is the most compelling. You could argue that the more-specific examples might turn away readers who don't want to read about bacteria, but, in the end, you want to reach as many *qualified* readers as possible; that is, readers who are interested in your subject.

- **Urgent**. Readers tend to save articles to read later. They email stories to themselves, paste links into Evernote, click Save Link in Facebook, and so on. If your headline makes a reader save your article to read later, then you've done something right. But life gets in the way and readers don't always return to those saved reads. The best way to get a reader to read your article is to get them to read it *now*, and the best way to do that is to convince them there's information within it that can't wait:

Here's the Simple Mistake You're Making With Your Taxes

One 'Bad Apple' Hire Can Damage Your Company Financially

Be Concise

I have only made this letter longer because I have not had the time to make it shorter.

–Blaise Pascal

Pascal is stating what every writer learns the hard way—it's easier to write long than to write short. Headlines pose a challenge: how do you accurately and interestingly sum up an entire story in only a few words? Keep your headlines as concise and efficient as possible. Long headlines muck up the page design and are hard on the eyes. Readers should be able to absorb an entire headline and its meaning in a quick glance, without stumbling over awkward phrasing and wordy construction. Use short words instead of long ones (write "use," not "utilize"). Don't use two words when one will suffice. Let's cut the following two headlines down to size:

If You Want to Resolve a Conflict Between Two People, You Really Need to Listen

5 Reasons to Implement an Instagram Strategy for Your Business

The concise versions are:

The Secret to Managing Conflict? Listen.

5 Reasons Your Business Should Be on Instagram

Suppose that you're writing a headline for an article citing studies about how humor affects consumer behavior. A sturdy, accurate headline is:

How Does Humor Affect Consumer Behavior? These Studies Show You

That's a little long and dry, so make it shorter and punchier:

That's clear and straightforward, but a bit wordy. If you're writing about humor, then you can be a little playful:

A Laughing Matter: Using Humor in Marketing

A short pun that sets the tone is followed by a concise, no-frills description of the content.

Be Engaging

Every good story has natural drama built into it, whether it's about the inescapable fate of star-crossed lovers or an office worker jumping through bureaucratic hoops trying to get a standing desk for his cubicle. A compelling tale has two or more forces acting in opposition to each other, and the tension that results from that struggle. If the story writer has done his or her job, and you may be the writer or you may be tasked with writing a headline for another writer's story, then it should be clear by reading the story—or even just the beginning of the story—what that drama is. If the story leaves the reader hanging or lacks obvious tension or excitement, then the headline writer needs to hunt for it, draw it out, and slap it boldly atop the story to capture the attention of readers. Headlines that grab a reader's attention usually involve one or more of the following elements:

- **Conflict.** Readers are drawn to the inherent drama in a battle, whether it's a battle between neighbors, nations, or brands of soft drink. For example:

    The 4 Business Skills Recruiters Are Looking for—and Not Finding

    This headline sets up conflict by showing that recruiters can't find what they need, and this topic is especially compelling to readers who may be looking for work.

- **Prominence.** Familiarity draws readers in. We like to read about famous people, popular brands, and well-known places. Look for familiar names, faces, and places in the story and use them in your headline. For example:

> 5 Amazing Visual Effects from Mad Max: Fury Road

- **Timeliness** It's not enough to tell your readers why they need to know something. You must tell them why they need to know it *now*. Consider adding words or phrases like "right now," "this week," or "today." For example:

    > Why is Poke So Hot Right Now? Here Are 9 Restaurants You'll Want to Try

    > 10 Things You Need to Know Today

Be Vibrant

Your headline sets the tone for the story that follows. If the headline's words are commonplace and predictable, then readers will assume that so is the accompanying story. Few people would bother to read articles titled:

> This Sports Car Is Really Fast

> How to Make Your Living Room Look Better

Here are some tips for writing headlines that hum with energy:

- **Choose surprising words over obvious ones.** Let's enliven the following straightforward but dull headlines:

    > The Vinyl Record Trend, Explained

    > Tips for Business Presentations

    A bit of wordplay yields conversational oomph:

    > Why Vinyl Records Are Back for Another Spin!

    > 11 Ways to Nail Your Next Presentation

- **Use alliteration.** Readers like words that repeat the same sounds. Why? Beats me. Few readers read headlines aloud. Perhaps readers subconsciously recognize that the headline writer has made an effort to be clever and trusts that the story will be entertaining as well. Listen for the sound repetition in the following examples:

How to Be a Better Blogger

Don't Fear the Gear: Packing for Patagonia

- **Play on familiarity.** Play on a familiar phrase or turn a popular title on its end. Again, you're playing on "we love what we know" psychology. For example:

Retro Recliners: Still Lazy After All These Years

The Grass Is Always Browner During a Drought

The Drench That Stole Christmas

Of course, playful language isn't always appropriate. If your story subject is serious, involving a crime or a sad turn of events, then a fun headline will usually backfire. You might also want to steer clear of wordplay for stories involving religion, race, gender inequality, and other sensitive topics.

Use Punchy Verbs

Action makes a story, and verbs bring action to any sentence or phrase. Verbs drive your headline and give life to the rest of the words. For example:

Accused Thief Takes the Stand

Top Cosmetics Company Cuts 2400 Jobs

Video Game Champ Leaves College for Sponsorship Deal

- **Use strong verbs.** Including a punchy verb is a smart and easy way to inject life into your headline. Always opt for specific verbs that describe a single action rather than ambiguous verbs that can mean any number of things. For example:

Miller Gets $1000

The verb "gets" is weak because it can mean too many things. Be specific:

Miller Wins $1000

Miller Steals $1000

Miller Borrows $1000

Miller Finds $1000

Other weak verbs to avoid include "is," "are," "can," "will," and "may." Instead, opt for strong, descriptive, punchy verbs like "insist," "delay," "strive," "cease," and "extend."

- **Don't make verbs into nouns**. Scan for trite phrases that make verbs out of nouns, and flip them back to their shorter, simpler, verb forms. These forms are less fussy, easier on the reader's eyes, and fit better in a small headline space. For example:

    Held a Meeting → Met
    Put in an Appearance → Appeared
    Reached an Agreement → Agreed
    Submitted His Resignation → Resigned
    Take Into Consideration → Consider

- **Use the active voice**. The active voice can make almost any headline a little more compelling. The active voice straightforwardly puts the doer at the beginning of the headline. For example:

    Company Slashes 15% of Workforce

    Man Dresses as Zebra, Breaks into Zoo

The opposite, the passive voice, shifts the doer later in the headline, sometimes awkwardly. For example:

    Workforce Slashed 15% by Company

    Zebra Costume Worn, Zoo Broken into by Man

Be Accurate

It's not hard to get a reader's attention in a world of information over-load—just say outrageous things:

    Safest Investment Trick: Consult a Psychic

Your Friends May Actually Hate You

The U.S. Is Overeducating Its Kids

The more outrageous your headline, the more attention you'll get. People *will* click. The problem with clickbait headlines, however, is that the articles they lead to don't live up to the drama that they promise. They leave the reader irritated or disappointed with the story, the writer, your website, your brand, and so on. And once you've lost a reader's trust, it's nearly impossible to regain it.

Your headline is your calling card. It sets the tone for the content that follows. If your headline isn't trustworthy, then your content is unreliable, meaning it's of literally no value. If your sole goal is to generate clickthroughs via clickbait headlines, and you don't care about duping your readers, then feel free to exaggerate and mislead. But if you believe that your content has something valuable to say, and you respect your readers and want them to return, then your goal is to nab readers' attention without lying or even fudging.

Suppose that you want to rewrite the headline for an article that's currently titled:

Conversations in Video Editing

The article features cutting-room anecdotes, workflow tips, and scene breakdowns by highly regarded video editors. They're not Oscar winners, but they've worked on high-profile shows—shows that you've heard of. Based on what you've learned so far about bringing the most compelling elements to light to halt readers in their tracks, you might be tempted to write a headline like:

Making the Cut: Behind the Scenes on TV's Top Series

That headline is compelling. It pokes at the base part of the brain that wants dirt, wants celebrity, wants in on something otherwise unseen. But it's inaccurate. The people who click it will find a nerdy, gossip-free article about video editors at a public-television news show and a children's network. They're going to be disappointed and lose all interest in the article. The readers lose and the writers lose.

The best headlines don't sacrifice substance for style. Your goal is to attract the people who really will be interested in the article. Here, that group is people who delight in the craft and technical minutia of professional video editing. Make the headline snappy, intriguing, and, above all, truthful:

Top Video Editors Share Their Storytelling Secrets

Trendy Headlines

Experiment with popular headline trends. If one suits your material, then try it to see whether it generates more clickthroughs than usual. If your platform lets you randomly present readers with alternate headlines to see which one gets the most clicks, called A/B testing (*wikipedia. org/wiki/A/B_testing*), then test two different headlines for the same article. A/B testing can yield invaluable insights into your audience. Keep in mind that trends become trends because they work, but readers eventually get wise to them. Be judicious. Here are some popular types of headlines:

- **Listicles.** One of the most popular forms of headline is the listicle (a portmanteau derived from *list* and *article*):

  9 Reasons to Binge-Watch 'The Mandalorian' This Weekend

  14 Surprising Ways to Make Kale Delicious

  5 Things You Didn't Know About Your Own Belly Button

  Often associated with Buzzfeed (*buzzfeed.com*), this trend exploded and was popular for years before it started to wane in major media outlets. Despite criticism that blames them for shortened attention spans and other societal maladies, listicles are effective because they promise a scannable narrative structure. Readers know what they're getting before they commit.

- **Informal headlines.** Lots of websites and blogs headline in a willfully informal style. In contrast to the headlines of traditional newspapers, informal headlines read like they've been lifted from a friendly chat:

  Raise Your Hand If You Hate This New Logo

Beige Smoothie Trend Is Just ... Eww

- **Question headlines**. A question headline sets up a need-to-know situation that the reader must click for the answer:

    A Text a Day to Keep the Doctor Away?

    It's easy to see why such questions generate clickthroughs. However, the adage known as Betteridge's Law of Headlines, named after a British technology journalist, states, "Any headline that ends in a question mark can be answered with the word *no*." Most readers have figured out that headlines that end in a question mark are usually peddling something that's not true:

    Could This Pill Be the End to the Common Cold?

    Has Disney Finally Met Its Match?

    Is a College Education a Thing of the Past?

    If you're going to pose a question in your headline, then make sure that the reader can't easily dismiss it with a "no" and move on. The questions posed by the following headlines should lead to a credible, in-depth response:

    Leaders vs. Managers: Which One Are You?

    What's You're Learning Style? Discover It—and Use It

    Which Ebook Distributor Is Right for You?

- **Tease headlines**. Headline writers know that readers have a hard time resisting a headline that keeps them guessing and promises instant gratification. A tease headline tells readers just enough to make them curious, and then forces them to click through to solve the mystery. Dirty trick? Yes. Effective? Yes. For example:

    You're About to Hate Slack as Much as You Hate Email

    Here's the Strange Bad News In the Latest Jobs Report

    This Stick of Butter Was Left Out At Room Temperature; You Won't Believe What Happens Next.

The final example is now so clichéd that it's become a parody of itself. What happens next is that your readers move on to another website because you can't think of a fresh way to get their attention.

Capitalizing Headlines

After you know what your headline is going to say, you must decide what it will look like. Consider the rest of your pages or publication's design standards. Are you going for the formal, traditional look of, say, the New York Times (*nytimes.com*)? Or a casual, modern look of, say, Mashable (*mashable.com*)?

- **Title case.** Traditionally formatted headlines are typed in title case, meaning they look like the title of a work of art, song, book, or movie. In other words, all the major words in the headline, or title, are capitalized. For example:

  Thunderstorm Kicks off Film Festival with a Boom

  In title case, most conjunctions, articles, and prepositions aren't capitalized. These small words include *a, the, or, if, but, and, on, in, of,* and, in this example, *off* and *with*. Note that all verbs, even small verbs, are capitalized. In the following title-cased headline, *in* and *the* aren't capitalized, but the verb *is* is capitalized:

  New Moon-Landing Movie Is in the Works

- **Sentence case.** A headline in sentence case looks like a normal sentence: the first letter of the first word is capitalized and all the subsequent words are in lower case. It's not unusual for traditional newspapers to use sentence-case headlines in their online editions, even if they use title-case headlines in their print editions. Here's the earlier headline in sentence case:

  Thunderstorm kicks off film festival with a boom

  Even in sentence case, you still must capitalize all proper nouns. Proper nouns (as opposed to common nouns) include names of people, titles, pets, places, businesses, institutions, languages, religions, brands, months, holidays, and specific or unique events. In the following examples, "Telluride Film Festival" and "Supreme Court" are proper nouns:

> Thunderstorm kicks off Telluride Film Festival with a boom

> Congress threatens to veto Supreme Court nominee

Whether you choose title case or sentence case, stick with it consistently to keep your blog or publication looking professional.

Punctuating Headlines

A well-placed period, em dash, comma, colon, or pair of single quotes can make your headline clearer and cleaner, infuse your headline with style and voice, and let you say more in a small space

- **Question mark (?)**. As mentioned earlier, posing a headline as a question can be a useful tool for engaging readers:

  > Has Congress Lost Their Ever-Loving Minds?

  > Is Binge-Watching, in Fact, Really Good for You?

- **Period (.)**. Headlines don't need a period. Here's an example of the same headline with and without a period; both are valid:

  > You'll Love These 5 Indonesian Roadside Delicacies

  > You'll love these 5 Indonesian roadside delicacies.

  A headline doesn't need a period, even when it's a complete sentence:

  > Baker Will Run for President

  However, you can use a period to offer structure and an assertive voice:

  > No, You Shouldn't Take Your Dog to Restaurants.

  > No, You Shouldn't Take Your Dog to Restaurants. Ever.

- **Em dash (—)**. An em dash sets off interrupting elements and calls attention to the interrupting material:

  > He Wanted Her Back—But Not This Way

The 5 Superfoods You're Not Eating—and Why

An em dash adds a little drama and rhythm to a headline, forcing the reader to slow down and hear it as a human voice, rather than see it as lifeless words on a page. Be sure not to use hyphens (-) when dashes (—) are called for.

- **Comma** (,). In headlines, the comma has a special power that it lacks in normal writing: it can replace the word "and," saving you space where you need it. For example, the following headline doesn't need an "and" between Mars and Jupiter because a comma is used:

    Scientists Send Rovers to Mars, Jupiter

- **Colon** (:). In addition to lending your headline a little gravitas, the colon also saves you space by letting you omit a word or two. For example, let's rewrite the following headline:

    Sconut Is the Next Incarnation in Donut Evolution

    You can use a colon to replace a word ("is") and give the headline dramatic build by flipping the order of ideas:

    Next Incarnation in Donut Evolution: The Sconut

- **Single quotes** (' '). When using quotation marks in a headline, the Associated Press and many other news organizations recommend single quotes (' ') instead of double quotes (" "). Single quotes save space and look more elegant in the large type sizes in which headlines typically run. Use quotation marks to quote someone directly, to set titles apart from regular text, or to give a phrase with a bit of a wink:

    'I'm Sorry,' Says Prime Minister

    Jump-Roping Toddler to Appear on 'Ellen'

    Chocolate Is Natural 'Truth Serum'

    Never use quotation marks to emphasize a word or phrase.

Writing Subheads

A single headline is often inadequate to describe a long or complex article. If a story contains varied important elements, then a subhead (subordinate headline) may be called for. (In journalism, a subhead is also called a deck.) A subhead:

- Appears below the main headline

- Is formatted in a smaller type size or a less-bold typeface

- Offers additional or crucial information that expands on the main headline

- Is another place to use SEO keywords (page 50) to gain the attention of search engines

The main headline grabs the reader's attention with broad ideas, and the subhead goes into detail to complete the picture:

> Remember Boredom?
> Research Shows Smartphone Habits Are Changing How Our Brains Work

> Shopping for Stun Guns
> 'Damsel in Defense' Replaces Tupperware as Latest Home Party Craze

> Tracking Your Teen with Tech
> Should Mom and Dad Be Playing Big Brother?

After you've gotten into the habit of writing concise headlines, having another entire headline to play with feels like a luxury. It may be tempting to be less stringent with the extra space, but continue to be economical with your language. Subheads shouldn't repeat anything that's in the headline. Instead, you want to doubly fascinate readers by essentially giving them two headlines to pique their interest.

The only difference between a headline and a subhead is that the subhead doesn't have to stand on its own. You can assume that readers have already read the main headline. For example:

> Backyard Chickens a Fowl Idea?
> The Downside of the Suburban Coop-Keeping Trend

The subhead doesn't repeat the word "chickens" because the headline has already established that the story is about chickens. Instead, the subhead refers to the established idea (chickens) while offering more information: coop-keeping is a trend in suburban areas and there's a downside.

Subheads have another use: they can be embedded throughout the article itself as dividers that lead off various sections of the story. Used in this way, subheads break up a long article visually, preventing the story from appearing as an intimidating wall of text. This practice, sometimes called chunking a story, divides the text into palatable bits. In the following example, subheads are used to break a long article into four sections:

> Why Vinyl Records Are Back for Another Spin
> *article text …*
>
> Is vinyl really better?
> *article text …*
>
> Getting creative
> *article text …*
>
> Consider the downsides
> *article text …*

The short phrases in these subheads help readers process long stories by priming them for, or offering a brief preview of, what they're about to read as they reach each new section. Readers can scan the subheads for the content that interests them. When you use subheads in this way, treat them like mini-headlines, subjecting them to the same considerations of content, style, and mechanics as normal headlines (except don't add subheads to subheads).

Using SEO Keywords

In addition to catching the reader's eye and conveying content, headlines should help readers find articles via search engines. Search engines such as Google, Bing, and Yahoo scour the web for keywords, index them, and present them in search results to readers. Headlines are one of the main places that search engines look to determine the content of a webpage. Think carefully about which keywords or key phrases you put in your headline, and even where you place them within the headline.

Keep in mind that while readers may appreciate wit and style, search engine algorithms certainly do not. If headline writing is considered to be both an art and a science, then keyword choice and placement is the science part. SEO (search engine optimization) is the process of affecting the visibility of a website or a webpage in a search engine's unpaid results. Two of the best SEO tools for researching keywords are Google Keyword Planner (*ads.google.com/home/tools/keyword-planner*), to get keyword ideas and statistics, and Google Trends (*trends.google. com*), to see what's being searched for around the world.

Another way to come up with keywords is to think like a searcher. If you were a reader and wanted to find a story like the one you're about to publish, what words would you type into Google to locate it? You wouldn't type a pun or "you won't believe what happens next." You'd type the phrase at the heart of the story. Those are your keywords.

After you decide on your keywords or key phrases, include them in your headlines and subheads so that search engines will find them and present your story to readers. Note the highlighted keywords in the following headlines:

Six Steps to Better **One-on-One Meetings**

The Making of a **Comic Book Page**: Start to Finish

The Pros and Cons of the **Canon EOS 5DS**

Search-engine results show only the first fifty or so characters of a headline, so place keywords at the beginning of the headline if possible. You can use a colon to move a key phrase to the front of a headline:

The **Canon EOS 5DS**: Pros and Cons

Online Research Tips: Finding Reliable Resources on the Web

TripMode: Don't Blow Through Your Allotted Data While Traveling

Coding for Kids: Create Your Own Weather App!

Popular blogging platforms such as WordPress have basic, built-in SEO tools, and you can add SEO plugins for in-depth research. Popular SEO tools include Yoast SEO (*wordpress.org/plugins/wordpress-seo*), SEOPress (*wpbeginner.com/refer/seopress*), and All in One SEO Pack (*wordpress.org/plugins/all-in-one-seo-pack*). Even if you choose not to use SEO tools, you'll usually get great results if you simply place your story's common-sense keywords at or near the beginning of the headline.

More Headline Tips

- For a given story, don't be surprised if you spend half your writing time just creating the headline. After all, if you don't grab your reader there, then the rest doesn't much matter.

- Run randomized A/B tests (*wikipedia.org/wiki/A/B_testing*) on different versions of headlines.

- Use online tools such as CoSchedule Headline Analyzer (*coschedule. com/headline-analyzer*) to analyze your headlines.

- For tips on writing and marketing online content, see Copyblogger. com (*copyblogger.com*).

- Ultimately, the skill that will serve you best in writing headlines isn't writing, but reading. Pay attention to the headlines that you see on online news sites, in paper-and-ink magazines, and in the newsletters in your inbox. Notice what you're drawn to and what you skim over.

3　Choosing the Perfect Word or Phrase

Use a Dictionary

To progress in your control of **denotation**, or the dictionary meaning of words, it's essential that you consult a full-size dictionary or a collegiate dictionary (printed, online, or app). For online searches, you can use the define: operator in Google and other search engines to look up a word; type define:fabulous, for example, to find the definition of the word *fabulous*. Full-size dictionaries provide extensive coverage of the language for native speakers. Collegiate dictionaries generally contain fewer entries (and fewer definitions per entry) than their full-size counterparts, but typically contain additional material, such as geographical, political, or biographical information, that might be useful to students. Publishers of quality dictionaries include Merriam-Webster, Oxford University Press, Random House, HarperCollins, and Houghton Mifflin Harcourt. After you read the prefatory guide of a dictionary, which explains how to interpret its abbreviations, symbols, and order of placing entries, you'll be able to find most or all of the following types of information:

- spelling
- parts of speech
- definitions
- synonyms
- antonyms

- alternative forms

- pronunciation

- capitalization

- derivations

- usage levels

- syllable division

- principles of usage

- abbreviations

- symbols

- biographical and given names

- places and population figures

- weights and measures

To see what a college dictionary can and cannot do, look at *Merriam-Webster*'s entry under *fabulous*:

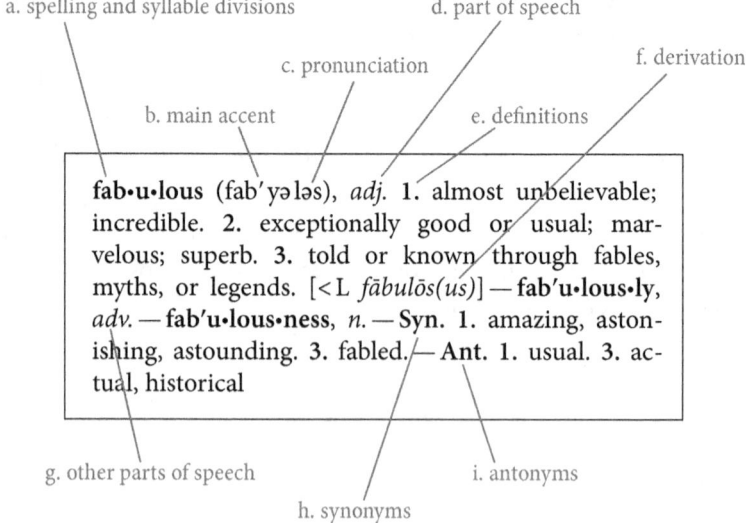

a. spelling and syllable divisions

d. part of speech

c. pronunciation

f. derivation

b. main accent

e. definitions

fab•u•lous (fab′yə ləs), *adj.* **1.** almost unbelievable; incredible. **2.** exceptionally good or usual; marvelous; superb. **3.** told or known through fables, myths, or legends. [<L *fābulōs(us)*] — **fab′u•lous•ly,** *adv.* — **fab′u•lous•ness,** *n.* — **Syn. 1.** amazing, astonishing, astounding. **3.** fabled. — **Ant. 1.** usual. **3.** actual, historical

g. other parts of speech

i. antonyms

h. synonyms

The entry shows, in the following order:

a. how the word is spelled and the points where syllable divisions occur (*fab•u•lous*)

    The lowercase *f* shows that *fabulous* isn't normally capitalized.

    If this word could be spelled correctly in different ways, then the less-common form would appear in a separate entry with a cross-reference to the more common form; thus the entry for *reenforce* merely sends you to *reinforce*. In your writing use the spelling under which a full definition has been given.

    Syllable division isn't completely uniform from one dictionary to another, but you cannot go wrong by following your dictionary's practice in every case. (You can also spare yourself trouble by not breaking up words at all; a little unevenness in right-hand margins is normal.)

b. where the main accent falls (*fab'*)

    If the word had another strongly stressed syllable like *hand* in *beforehand*, then you would find it marked with a secondary accent: *bi•for' hand'*.

c. how the word is pronounced

    The dictionary's pronunciation key reveals, among other things, that ə = *a* as in *alone*. (One dictionary's key will differ from another's.) Collegiate dictionaries make no attempt to capture regional or nonstandard pronunciations, like *noo' kul ər* for *noo' klē ər* (*nuclear*).

d. the **part of speech** (*adj.* for *adjective*)

    Some words, like *can* and *wait*, occupy more than one part of speech, depending on the context. Definitions are grouped according to those parts of speech. Transitive verbs (those that take an object) are usually listed separately from intransitive verbs (those that take no object). Thus dictionaries typically give all the intransitive senses of *wait* (*v.i.*), as in *Wait for me*, before the transitive senses (*v.t.*), as in *Wait your turn*!

e. three definitions of *fabulous*

No dictionary lists definitions in the order of their acceptability. The dictionary illustrated here begins with the most common part of speech occupied by a given word and, within each part of speech, offers the most frequently encountered meaning first. Some other dictionaries begin with the earliest meaning and proceed toward the present. The system used in your dictionary is clearly set forth in the prefatory material, which you should read through at least once.

f. the word's derivation from the first three syllables of the Latin word *fabulosus*

The derivation, or **etymology**, of a word is given only if its component parts are not obviously familiar—as they are, for example, in *freeze-dry* and *nearsighted*. Many symbols are used in stating etymologies; look for their explanation in the prefatory material of your dictionary.

g. an adverb and a noun stemming from the main word

Fabulously and *fabulousness* are "run-on entries," words formed by adding a suffix to the main entry.

h. synonyms of definitions 1 and 3

In most dictionaries a word with many apparent synonyms—words having the same or nearly the same meaning—is accompanied by a "synonym study" explaining fine differences. Thus, this dictionary's entry for *strength* concludes:

> — Syn. 4. STRENGTH, POWER, FORCE, MIGHT suggest capacity to do something. STRENGTH is inherent capacity to manifest energy, to endure, and to resist. POWER is capacity to do work and to act. FORCE is the exercise of power: *One has the power to do something. He exerts force when he does it. He has sufficient strength to complete it.* MIGHT is power or strength in a great degree: *the might of an army.*

This would be useful information if you were wondering which of the four similar words to use in a sentence. If you looked up *power*, *force*, or *might*, then you would find a cross-reference to the synonym study under *strength*.

i. antonyms (words with the opposite meaning) of definitions 1 and 3

If you're searching for a word to convey the opposite of a certain term, then check its listed antonyms. But if you're still unsatisfied, then look up the entries for the most promising antonyms and check their synonyms. This will greatly expand your range of choice.

So much for *fabulous*. But other sample entries would reveal still further kinds of information:

- *inflected forms.* Some entries show unusual inflected forms—that is, changes in spelling expressing different syntactic functions. You'll find unusual plurals (*louse, lice*); unusual principal parts of verbs (*run, ran*); pronoun forms (*I, my, mine*, and so on); comparative and superlative degrees of adjectives (*good, better, best*).

- *restrictive labels.* The entry will show how a word's use may be limited to a region (*Southern U.S., Austral., Chiefly Brit.*); to an earlier time or a kind of occasion (*Archaic, Obs., Poetic*); to a subject (*Bot., Anat., Law*); and most important for the writer, to a level of usage for words not clearly within standard American or British English (*Nonstandard, Informal, Slang*).

- *usage study.* Beyond its usage levels, your dictionary may offer especially valuable discussions of usage problems surrounding certain controversial words or meanings, such as *ain't, different from/than*, or *hardly* with negative forms:

> — Usage. HARDLY, BARELY, and SCARCELY all have a negative connotation, and the use of any of them with a supplementary negative is considered nonstandard, as in *I can't hardly wait* for *I can hardly wait.*

Master Idioms

An **idiom** is a fixed expression whose meaning cannot be deduced from its elements—for example, *put up with*, as in *She put up with his complaining*. For foreign students of English (or any other language), idioms are a continual source of worry. No amount of grammar study or knowledge of the separate meanings of *put*, *up*, and *with* will yield the right meaning; this idiom, like all others, must simply be learned as a unit. It isn't only foreigners, however, who stumble over idioms in their writing. Every reader is familiar with articles by native speakers who write *I was bored of being sick* or *in regards to traffic* (it should be *bored by* or *bored with* and *in regard to* or *with regard to*).

As these examples suggest, most of the mischief caused by idioms centers on prepositions—words like *down*, *up*, *in*, *out*, *by*, *of*, and *with*. What can you do to make sure that you're choosing the right preposition to go with a given expression? The answer is threefold:

1. Consult your dictionary; in many cases you'll find the idiom covered there.

2. Study the list of common idioms below.

3. Maintain a personal list of troublesome idioms, beginning with unfamiliar items in the following list and adding problem expressions that turn up in your writing.

Prepositions in Idioms

abide *by* a promise
abide *in* a place

acquiesce *in* a wish or request

adapt *from* a model
adapt *to* new conditions

affinity *with* a person

afraid *of* someone or something

agree *on* a strategy
agree *to* a proposal

agree *with* an opinion

analogy *with* something comparable
analogous *to* something comparable

angry *at* a situation
angry *with* a person

annoyed *with* or *by* a persistent bother or person

apropos *of* a topic

aptitude *for* a skill

at peace *with* oneself

in behalf of someone's interest
on behalf of someone absent

capacity *to* do something
capacity *of* that thing

charge *for* a purchase
charge *with* an offense

compare x *to* y [they are alike]
compare x *with* y [make the act of comparison]

concur *in* a judgment
concur *with* someone who has made a judgment

conform *to* a rule
in conformity *with* a rule

contend *for* a prize
contend *with* an obstacle or adversary

cooperate *with* authority

correspond *to* something equivalent
correspond *with* a letter writer

depart *from* tradition
depart *for* a destination

dependent *on* favors or persons

differ *about* or *over* an issue
differ *from* something different
differ *with* someone holding a contrary opinion

equal *to* something
equally *with* something

equivalent *to* a like case

fired *from* a job
fired *with* enthusiasm

free *from* interference or bondage
free *of* charge

frightened *by* something or someone

identical *to* or *with* something that is the same

impatient *at* a delay
impatient *for* a desired outcome
impatient *with* a person

independent *from* another country's rule
independent *of* support or supporting persons

inferior *to* something else

infer *from* a source

meet *with* an obstacle

oblivious *of* something forgotten
oblivious *to* an ignored circumstance

occupied *by* a tenant
occupied *in* deep thought
occupied (or preoccupied) *with* a concern

part *from* a friend
part *with* a possession

partake *of* a feast

participate *in* an activity

prior *to* something later

prohibit x *from* doing y

a report *of* an event
a report *on* a topic

rewarded *by* an outcome or person
rewarded *for* a good deed
rewarded *with* a prize

superior *to* something lesser

sympathy *for* the oppressed
sympathy *with* someone with like feelings

tired *of* an annoyance

wait *at* a bus stop
wait *for* a result
wait *on* a customer

Use Words in Established Senses

English is probably the fastest-changing of all languages, and yesterday's error often becomes today's standard usage. As a writer, however, you should be concerned not with anticipating shifts in taste but with communicating your ideas effectively. Many readers are upset by diction that is being used in some capricious or momentarily popular way. By being conservative in your choice of words, you can avoid arousing automatically negative responses to the content of your work. Many fad words have a common feature: they usually belong to one part of speech but are being used as another. Sometimes a suffix such as *-wise* or *-type* has been added to turn a noun into an adjective or adverb.

Gaswise, the car is economical. *(Bad)*

The car gets good mileage. *(Good)*

Preferencewise, she is looking for a **commuter-type** car. *(Bad)*

She wants a car suitable for commuting. *(Good)*

More often, one part of speech simply takes over another.

Faddish	Conservative
It was a **fun** party.	The party was **fun**.
She **authored** the book in 1989.	She **wrote** the book in 1989.
We **gifted** the newlyweds with a toaster.	We **gave** the newlyweds a toaster.
Mark is a **together** person.	Mark is a **confident, competent** person.
I would give anything for an **invite** to the party.	I would give anything for an **invitation** to the party.

The use of nouns as adjectives deserves special mention in an age of bureaucracy. Standard English allows many such **attributive nouns,** as they are called, as in *mountain time, night vision, cheese omelet,* and *recreation director.* But officials have a way of jamming them together in a confusing heap. A frugal governor, for example, once proposed what he called a *community work experience program demonstration project.* This row of nouns was meant to describe, or perhaps to conceal, a policy of getting welfare mothers to pick up highway litter without receiving any wages. As a writer, you would be wise to avoid changing the customary part of speech of a word or piling up attributive nouns.

Control Connotations

The prime requirement for controlling meaning is to know the denotations, or dictionary definitions, of the words you're using. But words also have important **connotations**—further suggestions or associations derived from the contexts in which the words have been habitually used. By and large, you won't find connotations in your dictionary; you have to pick them up from meeting the same words repeatedly in reading and conversation. Of course you can't expect to learn all the overtones of every English word. But as a writer you can ask yourself whether the words you've allowed into your first drafts are appropriate to the occasion. When you're unsure, think of related words until you find one that conveys the right associations.

Take, for example, the words *store*, *shop*, and *boutique*. Because of the contexts in which the words most often appear, they *connote* different things. When we think of a *store*, we picture an establishment where merchandise is sold. A *shop* suggests a smaller establishment selling a specific type of goods, or a department in a larger store, such as the *card shop* at Macy's. A *boutique* is a small shop that specializes in fashionable items, often clothing or accessories for women. If you were writing about the corner grocery that keeps your neighborhood in bread, milk, and other staples seven days a week, then you would want to call it a *store*. To call it a *shop* or a *boutique* would undercut your purpose in pointing out the establishment's diverse and ordinary stock.

Consider two further examples, *complex* versus *complicated* and *workers* versus *employees*. Although the members of each pair are close in denotation, their connotations differ. Suppose that you wanted to characterize an overelaborate instruction manual. Would you call it *complex* or *complicated*? I hope that you would choose *complicated*, which can imply not just intricacy but more intricacy than is called for. And if you were criticizing harsh factory conditions, then you would want to write about mistreated *workers*, not mistreated *employees*. These words denote the same people, yet *employees* characterizes them from a corporate point of view, whereas *workers* calls to mind laborers whose interests and loyalties may be quite different from those of the company.

Avoid using connotations too lopsidedly in favor of your own position on an issue. Suppose, for example, that you were writing an article about discourtesy among adolescents. If you chose the term *young thugs* to characterize teenagers, then you would certainly be making your feelings clear, but you would also be begging the question (reasoning in circles), forcing your reader to respond emotionally with you or against you. In revising your writing, tone down any inflammatory language that seems to convey ready-made conclusions.

Avoid Racist and Sexist Language

Because you're writing to convince, not to insult, nothing can be gained from using offensive terms. Racial slurs, demeaning stereotypes, and sexually biased phrases (*lady driver, typical male brutality*) make any fair-minded reader turn against the writer.

The problem of sexism in language deserves special discussion because it goes beyond any conscious wish to show prejudice. In recent decades people have been increasingly realizing that long-accepted conventions of word choice imply that women are inferior or are destined for restricted roles. To keep sexist language out of your prose, then, it's not enough to avoid grossly insulting terms; you must be watchful for subtler signs of condescension as well.

If, for example, you call William Shakespeare *Shakespeare*, then why should you call Emily Dickinson *Miss Dickinson* or, worse, *Emily*? Such names imply that a woman who writes poems isn't really a poet but a "poetess," a "lady poet," or even a "spinster poet." Write about *Dickinson's poetry*, thus giving it the same standing you would the work of any other author. Similarly, use *sculptor, lawyer,* and *nurse* for both sexes, avoiding such designations as *sculptress, lady lawyer,* and *male nurse*. And do without *coed*, which suggests that the higher education of women is an afterthought to the real (male) thing. Make your language reflect the fact that, in North America and Europe at any rate, men and women are now considered equally eligible for nearly every role.

Tact is necessary, however, in deciding how far to go in changing traditional expressions. The ideal is to avoid sexism without sacrificing clarity and ease of expression. If you wrote *actor* for *actress* and *waiter* for *waitress*, for example, then your readers would be confused; rightly or wrongly, common usage still recognizes separate terms for male and female performers of those functions. But when in doubt, choose a sex-neutral term: not *mankind* but *humanity*, not *man-made* but *artificial*.

The *-Person* **Suffix.** Try to find nonsexist alternatives to awkward *-person* suffixes, which sound ugly to many readers of both sexes.

Sexist	Nonsexist But Awkward	Preferable
chairman	chairperson	chair, head
Congressman	Congressperson	Representative
mailman	mailperson	letter carrier
policeman	policeperson	police officer
weatherman	weatherperson	meteorologist

Pronouns and Gender

Perhaps the sorest of all issues in contemporary usage is that of the so-called **common gender.** Which pronouns should you use when discussing an indefinite person, a "one"? Traditionally, that indefinite person has been "male": *he, his, him,* as in *A taxpayer must check his return carefully.* For the centuries in which this practice went unchallenged, the masculine pronouns in such sentences were understood to designate not actual men but people of either sex. Today, however, many readers find these words an offensive reminder of second-class citizenship for women. Remedies that have been proposed include using the phrase *he or she* (or *she or he*) for the common gender, treating singular common words as plural (*A taxpayer must check their return*), combining masculine and feminine pronouns in forms like *s/he,* and using *she* in one sentence and *he* in the next.

Unfortunately, all of these solutions carry serious drawbacks. Continual repetition of *he or she* is cumbersome and monotonous; many readers would regard *A taxpayer must check their return* as a blunder, not a blow for liberation; pronunciation of s/he is uncertain; and the use of *she* and *he* in close alternation, though increasingly common, risks confusing the reader by implying that two indefinite persons, a female and a male, are involved.

To avoid such awkwardness, follow these guidelines:

- Use *she* whenever you're sure the indefinite person would be female (a student in a women's college, for example):

  Someone who enters a nunnery must sacrifice everything from **her** former life.

- Don't use *she* for roles that have been "traditionally female" but are actually mixed: nurse, secretary, school teacher, laundry worker, and so forth. Female pronouns in such contexts imply an offensive prejudgment about "women's place." Use plural forms to show a sex-neutral attitude.

  A kindergarten teacher has **her** hands full every day. *(Bad)*

  Kindergarten teachers have **their** hands full every day. *(Good)*

- Use an occasional *he or she* or *she or he* to indicate an indefinite person:

  When a driver is stopped for a traffic violation, **he or she** would do well to remain polite.

  But be sparing with this formula; it can become annoying.

- Try, throughout a piece of writing, using *she* consistently as the "common gender" pronoun. Your reader will become quickly adjusted to the change, especially if you yourself are female.

- If your uses of the common gender are few and widely spaced, then try alternating the masculine and feminine forms.

- Avoid the singular whenever your meaning isn't affected.

  A taxpayer must check **his** return. *(Bad)*

  Taxpayers must check **their** returns. *(Good)*

- Omit the pronoun altogether whenever you can do so without awkwardness.

  Everyone needs **his or her** vacation. *(Acceptable)*

Everyone needs **a** vacation. *(Better)*

Avoid Jargon

Jargon is specialized language that appears in a nonspecialized context, thus giving a technical flavor to statements that would be better expressed in everyday words. When you're writing about, say, economics, anthropology, or psychology, you can and should use terms that are meaningful within the field: *liquidity, kinship structure, paranoid*, and so forth. But those same terms become jargon when used out of context.

> My **liquidity profile** has been weak lately. *(Jargon)*
>
> I've been short of **cash** lately. *(Ordinary term)*
>
> Her **kinship structure** extends from coast to coast. *(Jargon)*
>
> Her **family** is scattered from coast to coast. *(Ordinary term)*
>
> Roland was really **paranoid** about the boss's intentions. *(Jargon)*
>
> Roland was **suspicious** of the boss's intentions. *(Ordinary term)*

Most jargon today comes from popular academic disciplines such as sociology and psychology, from government bureaucracy, and from the world of computers. Here's some of the more commonly seen jargon, accompanied by everyday equivalents that would usually be preferable.

Jargon	Ordinary Term
access (v.)	enter, make use of
behaviors	acts, deeds, conduct
correlation	resemblance, association
cost-effective	economical
counterproductive	harmful, obstructive
dialogue (v.)	talk, converse
ego	vanity, pride
facilitate	help, make possible
feedback	response
finalize	complete

Jargon	Ordinary Term
input	response, contribution
interface (v.)	meet, share information with
maximize	make the most of
obsession	strong interest
parameters	borders
prioritize	prefer, rank
reinforcement schedule	inducements
sociological	social
syndrome	pattern
trauma	shock
user-friendly	uncomplicated

You can put jargon to good comic or ironic use, but when you find it appearing uninvited in your drafts, revise.

Aim for Middle Diction

Different situations call for different levels of diction (word choice), from the slang that may be appropriate in a letter to a friend, to the formal language expected in a legal document, to the technical terms demanded by a scientific report. But whenever you are writing outside such special contexts, you should aim for **middle diction**—language that is neither too casual to convey serious concern nor too stiff to express feeling.

The best way to recognize levels of diction is to be an observant reader of different kinds of prose and a close listener to conversations. But if you have studied Latin or a "Latinate" modern language such as Spanish, French, or Italian, then you have a head start toward spotting formal English diction. All the words in the right column in the following table are both formal and Latinate.

Slang	Middle Diction	Formal Diction
mug	face	visage
kicks	pleasure	gratification
threads	clothes	attire

Slang	Middle Diction	Formal Diction
specs	glasses	spectacles
rip off	steal	expropriate
big-mouthed	talkative	voluble

Deliberately Extreme or Mixed Diction

If you have a firm sense of diction levels and want to create an effect of irony, then you can do so by playing with fancy language or with slang. You can, for example, write a passage that uses a sentence structure and diction that are deliberately "high": *it's time to idly, in the manner of certain doges, select from the bounty of the earth some particularly fragrant and ornamental nutrition bundle, feather footed through the plashy fen passes the questing vole.* Such a style establishes a comic distance between the writer and his subject; he is winking at us and saying, "Is this stuff pretentious, or what?"

Similarly, you can achieve irony by nudging your reader with a combination of high and low language. The contrast between high-falutin words and slangy ones tips the reader that the writer's subject shouldn't be taken at face value.

Be Concrete

Concrete words name observable things or properties like *classroom* and *smoky*; **abstract** words convey ideas like *education* and *pollution*—nonphysical things that we can grasp only with our minds, not with our senses. Of course gradations exist between the extremes: a *university* is more concrete than *education* but less so than a *classroom*, a distinct physical place. The more concrete the term, the more vivid it will be to a reader.

Whenever you are describing something or telling a story, you can hardly go wrong by making your successive drafts more concrete. Suppose that you are trying to characterize your new keyboard, which you have praised in your first draft as *extremely modern*. That is an abstract judgment that could mean anything to anyone. What precisely is modern about the machine? In revising, think about the *LED backlighting, programmable macros, media controls, mechanical keyswitches, RGB indicator lights, type-C connection,* and so forth. Get the concrete details into your writing, convincing your reader that your general statements rest on observations.

Be Concise

Your reader's attention will depend in large part on the ratio between information and language in your prose. Wordiness, or the use of more words than are necessary to convey a point, is one of the most common and easily corrected flaws of style. The fewer words you can use without harm to your meaning, the better.

Wordy	Concise
among all the problems that exist today	among all current problems
an investment in the form of stocks and bonds	an investment in stocks and bonds
at the present time	now
due to the fact that	because
during the course of	during
for the purpose of getting rich	to get rich
for the simple reason that	because
in a very real sense	truly
in spite of the fact that	although
in the not too distant future	soon
in view of the fact that	since
it serves no particular purpose	it serves no purpose
majoring in the field of astronomy	majoring in astronomy
my personal preference	my preference
on the part of	by
owing to the fact that	because
proceeded to walk	walked
rarely ever	rarely

Wordy	Concise
seldom ever	seldom
the present incumbent	the incumbent
to the effect that	that

Avoiding Redundancy

A **redundancy** is an expression that conveys the same meaning more than once—for example, *circle around*, which says "go around around." The difference between writing *She circled the globe* and *She circled around the globe* is that in the second version the word *around* delivers no new information and thus strains the reader's patience.

Examine your drafts to see whether they contain redundancies, and be uncompromising in pruning them.

Redundant	Concise
adequate enough	adequate
advance planning	planning
both together	both
but yet	but
contributing factor	factor
deliberate lie	lie
equally as far	as far
exact same	same
few in number	few
final outcome	outcome
free gift	gift
join together	join
large in size	large
past experience	experience
past history	history
refer back	refer
set of twins	twins

Redundant	Concise
share in common	share
shuttle back and forth	shuttle
two different	two

Redundancy also occurs when you unnecessarily repeat an expression that may not be redundant in itself. Every writer has favorite words that tend to get overused in the course of writing. Reread your drafts to ferret out such terms, and consult your dictionary or thesaurus if necessary to explore alternative ways of conveying the same meaning.

When you suspect that you have been using a certain expression too often, run a "Find All" search for that term in your word processor or editor, and revise accordingly.

Avoiding Circumlocution

All redundancies fall into the broader category of **circumlocutions**—that is, roundabout forms of expression. But some circumlocutions, instead of saying the same thing twice, take several words to say almost nothing. Formulas like *in a manner of speaking* or *to make a long story short*, for example, are simply ways of making a short story long. Watch especially for cumbersome verb phrases like *give rise to*, *make contact with*, and *render inoperative*; prefer *arouse, meet, destroy*. And if you mean *because*, don't reach for *due to the fact that*. When five words do the work of one, all five are anemic.

Circumlocution	Concise Expression
He was of a kindly nature.	He was kind.
It was of an unusual character.	It was unusual.
My father and I have differences about dating.	My father and I differ about dating.
I finally made contact with my supervisor.	I finally met my supervisor.
The copy that is pink in color is for yourself.	Keep the pink copy.

Circumlocution	Concise Expression
She suspected she would be in an unemployment-type kind of situation when the overflow of customers due to the Christmas shopping circumstances was no longer in effect.	She suspected she would be laid off after the Christmas rush.

Prune Intensifiers

In conversation most of us use intensifiers—"fortifying" words like *absolutely, basically, certainly, definitely, incredibly, intensely, just, of course, perfectly, positively, quite, really, simply, so, too,* and *very*—without pausing to worry about their meaning. And in telling stories or expressing opinions, we veer toward the extremes of *fantastic, terrific, sensational, fabulous,* and *awful, horrible, terrible, dreadful.* Our listeners know how to allow for such exaggeration. Most written prose, however, aims at a more measured tone. Look through your drafts for intensifiers, and see how many of them you can eliminate without subtracting from your meaning. Your revised work will not only be more concise and therefore less taxing to read, it will also sound more assured. Readers sense that intensifiers are morale-building words meaning *maybe* or *I hope*; doing without such terms is a sign of your confidence that you are making a sound case for your ideas.

Put Statements in Positive Form

Negative ideas are just as legitimate as positive ones; you may have to point out that something did not happen or that an argument leaves you unconvinced. But the negative modifiers *no* and *not* sometimes make for wordiness and a slight loss of readability. If you write *We are not in agreement,* then you are asking your reader to go through two steps, first to conceive of agreement and then to negate it. But if you simply write *We disagree,* then you have saved three words and simplified the mental operation. The gain is small, but good writing results from a sum of small gains.

Of course you need not develop a phobia against every use of *no* or *not*. Observe, however, that negatively worded sentences tend to be slightly less emphatic than positive ones.

Negative	Positive
She did not do well on the test.	She did poorly on the test.
He was not convicted.	He was acquitted.
They have no respect for rationing.	They despise rationing.
It was not an insignificant amount.	It was a significant amount.

Avoid Euphemisms

A **euphemism** is a squeamishly "nice" expression standing in the place of a more direct one. Some words that began as euphemisms, such as *senior citizen* and *funeral director*, have passed into common usage, but you should try to avoid terms that still sound like ways of covering up a meaning instead of conveying it. Euphemisms often conceal a devious political or commercial motive. If you want to be regarded as candid and trustworthy, then don't write *discomfort* for *pain*, *memory garden* for *cemetery*, *pass away* for *die*, *relocation center* for *concentration camp*, *revenue enhancement* for *tax raise*, *adult* for *pornographic*, *deployment of forces* for *invasion*, and so forth.

Euphemistic	Direct
The governor is extremely concerned about human resources development.	The governor is extremely concerned about unemployment.
The candidate issued a press release declaring that her earlier remarks about her opponent were now to be considered inoperative.	The candidate issued a press release admitting that her earlier remarks about her opponent were untrue.
We are recalling all late models because the bearings at variance with production code specifications may adversely affect vehicle control.	We are recalling all late models because the defective bearings may cause drivers to lose control of the steering.

Avoid Clichés

A **cliché** is a trite, stereotyped, overused expression such as *throw money around* or *bring the house down*. Clichés are **dead metaphors**—that is, they are figures of speech that no longer sound figurative. When someone writes *off the wall* or *the bottom line*, no reader sees a wall or a line. On the other hand, a writer could blunder into causing people to see real bricks by saying *On the first day that June worked in the construction crew, Steve fell for her like a ton of bricks* (an accidentally revived cliché). But the usual effect of clichés is not unintended comedy but simple boredom. The reader feels that the writer is settling for prepackaged language instead of finding the exact words to convey a particular thought. And matters are not improved by the apologetic addition of *so to speak* or *as the saying goes*. When you need to apologize for any expression, change it.

The worst thing about cliché-ridden prose is its predictability. As soon as we register one element of the cliché, the rest of it leaps to mind like an advertising jingle:

> pleasingly ... plump
>
> lines of ... communication
>
> the foreseeable ... future
>
> the pieces ... of the puzzle ... fall into place

The resultant prose—*to be brutally honest*—is a *far cry* from being a *sure winner* in the *hearts and minds* of readers *from every walk of life*.

Three lists of clichés follow. List A includes examples of gross clichés, which you can spot fairly easily and eradicate as you revise. List B includes less obvious clichés, pairs of seemingly inseparable adjectives and nouns, clusters that choke out your originality as a writer. List C consists of pat expressions that say too little in a wordy and predictable manner.

List A: Gross Clichés
> a needle in a haystack
> blind as a bat

carve a niche for oneself
drive one to distraction
happy as a lark
live like a king
make a beeline for
old as the hills
one in a million
quiet as a mouse
rule with an iron fist
sly as a fox
smart as a whip
sow one's wild oats
the top of the heap
tough as nails

List B: "Inseparable" Pairs
bounce back
flawless complexion
grave danger
high spirits
integral part
nuclear holocaust
supreme moment
tempestuous affair
tender mercies
unforeseen obstacles
vicious circle
vital role

List C: Pat Expressions
after all is said and done
at this point in time
far be it from me
in a very real sense
in the final [last] analysis
in this day and age

it goes without saying
it stands to reason
once and for all
when push comes to shove

Watch for Distracting Sound Patterns

Knowing that repeated sounds draw attention, you can sometimes use them deliberately, as Mark Twain did in referring to

the **calm confidence** of a **Christian** with four aces,

or as Thomas Paine did in writing

These are the **times** that **try** men's souls.

In these examples the "poetic" quality goes along with the effort to make a concisely emphatic statement.

Unless you are after some such effect, however, beware of making your reader conscious of rhymes (*the side of the hide*) or alliteration (*pursuing particular purposes*) or repeated syllables (*apart from the apartment*). These snatches of "poetry" usually result from an unconscious attraction that words already chosen exert on subsequent choices. Having written *the degradation*, you write *of the nation* because the *-ation* sound is in your head. You may have to read your first draft aloud, attending to its sound and not its sense, in order to find where you have lapsed into jingling.

Abstract Latinate words—the ones that usually end in *-al, -ity, -ation,* or *-otion*—are especially apt to make a repetitive sound pattern. It's worth the pains to rewrite, for example, if you find bunched words like *functional, essential, occupational,* and *institutional* or *equality, opportunity, parity,* and *mobility.*

Experiment With Understatement and Hyperbole

Language that conspicuously minimizes an extreme state of affairs can also be regarded as figurative, even if it doesn't draw a comparison. Thus imaginative effects are at work in the following examples of **understatement**:

You get **a little sweaty** out there fighting a forest fire.

To be born with a cocaine addiction is **not necessarily the most advantageous way to enter the world.**

She worked at the office from nine until five, endured a second rush-hour traffic jam, cooked the dinner, and rushed off to the emergency room with her suddenly feverish child—**just a routine day in the life of a single mother.**

Similarly, you can get a figurative effect through **hyperbole,** or overstatement:

He entered the limousine, sucking imperiously on a **torpedo-sized cigar.**

They won't do a thing about smokestack pollution **until the view from their penthouses is a solid wall of soot.**

The moths on the Puerto Vallarta coast **were as big as B-52s, and the cockroaches looked like Winnebagos.**

"'Mind if I smoke?' might once have been a rather routine query. **Today it's about the same as China asking, 'Mind if I drop in?'**"

As you can see, understatement and hyperbole produce an effect of **irony,** or the conveying of something quite different from what one's words seem to say. Like other successfully handled figures of speech, these devices tell the reader that the writer has been confident enough to play with language while still maintaining rhetorical control. The effect would be ruined, of course, if it were carried through an entire serious article.

Use Unstrained Similes and Metaphors

Two closely related figures of speech let you draw imaginative likenesses. A **simile,** by including the word *like* or *as*, explicitly acknowledges that a comparison is being made.

Like a patio rotisserie, Tom's mind always keeps turning at the same slow rate, no matter what is impaled on it. *(Simile)*

Tom's mind is explicitly compared to a rotisserie.

A **metaphor** omits *like* or *as.*

> Tom's hedgeclipper mind gives a suburban sameness to everything it touches. *(Metaphor)*

Tom's mind is compared to hedgeclippers, but without either of the explicit terms of comparison, *like* or *as.*

In theory a metaphor is a more radical figure of speech than a simile, for it asserts an identity, not just a likeness, between two things (Tom's mind "is" a gardening tool). But in practice one kind of figure can be as striking as the other. What counts is not the choice between simile and metaphor but the suitability of the image to your intended meaning. The two images about Tom, for example, call to mind not only his conformism but also his specifically suburban background (the carefully tended hedge, the patio rotisserie).

Simile and metaphor are among the most common figures of speech.

Similes

> I ate until I was **as** stuffed **as** a taxidermist's owl.

> Seeing Tina Turner onstage is **like** watching a demented child who stamps her feet, twirls in circles, and bops around bow-legged **as though** she's wearing a diaper.

> It is **like** sharing an aquarium with a very large ocean-going predator of uncertain appetite.

Metaphors

> The primary Whitman ... opened a new circuit between the energies of sensuality and the energies of language, making them the electric poles of his identity.

> Chicago's rising star is now a worn-out supernova, which has exploded all over suburbia.

> Dying leaves and dead Red Sox—that's the New England autumn.

When a simile or metaphor succeeds, it usually bears a stamp of naturalness and transparency; the reader can immediately see through the chosen figure to the intended resemblance. Consider, for instance, the image (highlighted) that concludes this paragraph (Felix Rohatyn, 1990):

> *The ideals of the revolutions in Poland, Hungary, Czechoslovakia, and even Bulgaria owe much to the American model, with its combination of political freedom and an economic system that seems to guarantee an ever-rising standard of living. It is important to recognize that it is a version of American political democracy, and not Japanese discipline or German efficiency, that the new leaders of these countries say they are striving for. Whether and how they will succeed is impossible to predict; their struggle will be long and may not always be peaceful. It is worth examining, however, whether the American system is all that they think it is, or whether **they are seeing the light of a distant star which, some time ago, may have ceased to shine so brightly.***

This writer, believing that the American socioeconomic system has entered a hard period and knowing that eastern Europeans have little accurate knowledge of our present condition, wonders whether their ideas about us aren't obsolete. If so, the metaphor says, perhaps what the Poles, Czechs, and others see in the American way is comparable to what all people see in a star—a light given off long ago, before the star itself began to fade. The image appears precisely and effortlessly suited to the thought behind it.

Occasionally, however, instead of looking uncontrived, a successful figure of speech will startle us with its boldness. Only after a double-take do we realize that the image is not just fresh but also apt. Consider this passage, written by a literary journalist (Anatole Broyard, 1990) who knew that he had only weeks to live and who longed for good conversation with his taciturn doctor:

> *Whether he wants to be or not, the doctor is a storyteller, and he can turn our lives into good or bad stories, regardless of the diagnosis. If my doctor would allow me, I would be glad to help*

him here, to take him on as my patient. Perhaps later, when he is older, he'll have learned how to converse. Astute as he is, he doesn't yet understand that all cures are partly "talking cures." **Every patient needs mouth-to-mouth resuscitation, for talk is the kiss of life.**

Here two metaphors are combined daringly. The first one startles us by seeming to be bizarrely literal; *what do you mean*, we want to protest, *"every patient needs mouth-to-mouth resuscitation"?* Only when we have digested the second, plainly figurative, image of talk as the kiss of life do we realize that the other image is figurative as well: the mouth-to-mouth resuscitation being evoked is simply talk itself. Yet with this delayed insight the imaginative brilliance and deathbed eloquence of the whole sentence becomes apparent.

This example shows that careful writers can defy the English teacher's maxim that figures of speech should keep their distance from one another. For further evidence, look at this tightly controlled sequence of images (Annie Dillard, 1989):

When you write, you lay out a line of words. The line of words is a miner's pick, a woodcarver's gouge, a surgeon's probe. You wield it, and it digs a path you follow. Soon you find yourself deep in new territory. Is it a dead end, or have you located the real subject? You will know tomorrow, or this time next year.

In this passage one metaphor, the *line of words*, is subdivided into three others, the *pick*, the *gouge*, and the *probe*. And still the writer isn't through; her verbal tool *digs a path* leading to *new territory* that may or may not prove a *dead end*. The passage flirts with absurdity but survives, barely, by virtue of its cunning. All of those images work together to represent the point being made—that writing is a risk-taking enterprise that can lead anywhere, or in some cases nowhere.

The danger of **mixed metaphor** is not that images will rub shoulders but that they will take a pratfall together. And it arises not when writers deftly reconcile two or more figures but precisely when they fail to do so, allowing one image's implications to clash disastrously with the other's. Consider:

> A tiger in the jungle of politics, he was a cream puff around the
> house. *(Mixed metaphor)*

The reader's mind strains unsuccessfully to grasp how a *tiger* is mean-
ingfully related to a *cream puff*—that is, how a wild animal can be
changed into a dessert.

> A tiger in the jungle of politics, he was a pussycat around the
> house. *(Effective metaphor)*

The images of *tiger* and *pussycat* are closely related, and the writer
(characterizing his father-in-law, U.S. President Harry Truman) fully
controls the different implications of the two terms.

Again, note how the following paragraph jumbles several figures of
speech in this mixed metaphor:

> Although some analysts feel that the presidential primary sys-
> tem is the wrong game plan for choosing the best nominee,
> they forget that primaries are an important mirror and proving
> ground of our democracy. To be sure, candidates can get burned
> out on the hustings. But by diving into the very heart of state
> and county politics, the survivors of this pressure cooker can
> acquire a hands-on feeling for the people they hope to govern.

This passage begins with a sports metaphor, *game plan*, but before the
first sentence is over we have been taken through two more incompat-
ible images, a *mirror* and a *proving ground*. The next sentence tells us
that candidates can get *burned out on the hustings* (literally, speaking
platforms)—a mixed metaphor that unintentionally suggests a public
execution. And finally, those candidates who survive the *pressure cooker*
are said to be *diving into a heart* where they can get a *hands-on feeling*.
Emergency surgery in the kitchen? Clearly, this writer likes to reach
for the handiest figurative language without taking responsibility for
its implications.

Perhaps you feel that you can avoid mixed metaphors by shunning
figurative language altogether. But insofar as you do, your prose will
be flat and colorless. Besides, it's not really possible to be completely
unfigurative. Many ordinary terms and nearly all clichés are **dead**

metaphors—that is, they contain the faint implication of an image which we are not supposed to notice as such (the *leg* of a table, a *blade* of grass). When clichés are used in close succession, they mischievously come back to life as mixed metaphors:

> **Climbing to the heights** of oratory, the candidate **tackled** the issue.

> Either we **get a handle** on these problems or we are all **going down the drain.**

> You can't **sit on your hands** if a recession is developing, because **you don't know where the bottom is.**

Figurative language, then, can be tricky. When you intend an abstract meaning, you have to make sure that your dead metaphors stay good and dead. But when you do wish to be figurative, see whether your image is vivid, fresh, and consistent. Literal statement may be safe, but a striking figure carried through consistently can unify and intensify your sentences.

4 Marketing to Businesses

You have only a few seconds to make a good first impression, an impression that will set the tone for the rest of your relationship. This chapter uses plenty of examples to explain the proper use of etiquette in your emails, text messages, telephone calls, and business letters. These lessons will help you evaluate your own communications, strike the right tone, and ensure that your recipients won't misinterpret you.

- Learn which communication method to use and when.

- Make action items communicate the right level of urgency.

- Use the subject, greeting, and signature of your email to set the tone of the message.

- Acknowledge receipt of an email, use autoresponders, and follow up on unanswered email.

- Use Cc, Bcc, and Reply All correctly.

- Learn what and what not to say in a text message.

- Understand what to say over the telephone.

- Record phone greetings and out-of-office messages that are clear and effective.

- Leave the right voicemail message.

- Format business letters properly.

- Write appropriate thank-you notes, sympathy cards, and requests for payment.

- Know when to bend or break the rules based on your own situation.

Email

The Subject, Greeting, and Signature

The subject, greeting, and signature of your email set the tone of the message. Let's improve the following email sent to a prospective client:

```
Subject: Terrific Opportunity!

Hey, Alice!

I heard about this workshop and immediately thought
about you. This Thursday, May 14, at 6 PM, we'll be
hosting a free class on How to Start Your Own Podcast
at the Canterbury Hotel downtown.

If you'd like to attend free as my guest, please call
Ruth at 212-555-1234 to RSVP.

I hope this helps with those content marketing issues
you were talking about.

All the best,

Bob
212-555-9999
Dunham & Fry
```

The Subject Line. The subject "Terrific Opportunity!" says almost nothing about the content of the email, and won't help the recipient (Alice) find the email later. A better subject line would be:

```
Free Class: How to Start Your Own Podcast, May 14.
```

When you reply to an email, the original subject is prefixed with the label "Re:" automatically. If your reply expands the current topic, introduces a new topic, or otherwise veers away from the existing conversation, then you should change the subject line to reflect the new topic, or send a new email instead. No one wants an email listing like the following when not all the messages are actually about the office holiday party:

```
Re: Office holiday party (2:40 PM)

Re: Office holiday party (2:52 PM)

Re: Office holiday party (3:55 PM)

Re: Office holiday party (4:11 PM)

Re: Office holiday party (5:08 PM)
```

If any one of these emails discussed seating for Monday's all-hands meeting, for example, then you should start a new email with the subject line:

```
Seating for Monday's all-hands meeting
```

The Greeting. The greeting:

```
Hey, Alice!
```

most likely isn't appropriate for an email to a new prospect. The recipient could easily take offense at an overly familiar business greeting. If you're uncertain about the recipient's preference, then use a formal greeting like:

```
Dear Mrs. Alvarez,
```

If the email has multiple recipients, then address them as a group, such as:

```
Dear Marketing Team,
```

or order them individually by their status or position in the organization's hierarchy:

```
Dear Ms. Green, Mr. Warburton, and Mrs. Garner,
```

for a CEO, Vice President, and Manager respectively.

Tip: If you don't know whether a woman prefers to be addressed as Mrs., Miss, or Ms., then use the neutral salutation Ms.

Your Signature. Vary your signature depending on your position and the information that you want to convey. The signature in the example email above should provide more than the sender's first name, telephone number, and organization name.

In the first email of a conversation (also called a thread), the signature should include at a minimum:

- Your name. If you don't have a strong relationship with the recipient, then use both your first name and last name.

- Your phone number.

- Your email address. Although your email address is also included in the From section of the email, some email servers replace known email addresses with the person's name, meaning that either the recipient can't see your address or must take extra steps to view it. When you create a signature, you should assume that the recipient will copy and paste it into an address book:

Other information that you might want to include depending on your business is:

- Organization name
- Job title
- Website address
- Social media links
- Fax number
- Office address
- Organization description
- A brief announcement, slogan, or promotional phrase
- A small image

Tip: Some email clients and servers block images. If your name, telephone number, or email address are shown in the image, then repeat the information as text below the image, ensuring that your contact info isn't lost due to a non-displayed image.

Don't make your signature too long. List the most important information—your name and contact info—first. Here's an appropriate email signature for a first email message:

```
Bob Clay
Dunham & Fry, content marketing strategy and research
212-555-9999
bob.clay@DunhamAndFry.com

Follow us on Facebook at www.facebook.com/DunhamAndFry

Subscribe to our newsletter at www.DunhamAndFry.com
```

Tip: Don't use your full signature when replying to an email. Doing so makes the thread too long and too unwieldy to read easily. Instead, list only the basics: your name, telephone number, and email address. Your recipient will be able to find the most important information quickly without excessive scrolling.

The Message Body

The body of your email must convey your message clearly. Let's improve the following email sent to a prospective client:

```
Dear Ms. Smith,

I hope that you're doing well. The weather is unseasonably
warm here -- I hope that yours is cooler. It was nice
seeing you the other day and I look forward to working
with you. I have attached the estimate that you asked
for to this email. Send me your online advertising
budget and I'll add that to the summary page. Also,
please let me know whether you found the clickthrough
rate statistics that you were looking for. If not, I can
send you a referral. Let me know whether you have any
```

questions. I will be traveling for the next week, so I might be a little slow to respond. If you can't reach me, you can call Tammy in my office and she'll help you. Also, don't forget about the free workshop tomorrow night. It is 6-8 PM at the downtown Hyatt Regency. I hope that you can join us.

Thanks!

Bob

Most people don't read every word of an email. Instead, they skim for important information. The more "skimmable" your message, the more likely you'll get a response from an appreciative recipient. Here are a few ways to make your message more readable:

- Use bullet points for multiple pieces of information.

- Keep the email short by omitting filler words and irrelevant topics. One friendly sentence usually suffices.

- Use paragraph breaks and whitespace to separate key points or ideas.

- Add brief memory-jogging descriptions when referring to meetings, presentations, reports, and other people.

By applying these guidelines to the example email above, we get:

Dear Ms. Smith,

Attached is the content marketing estimate that you requested.

- Send me your online advertising budget and I'll add that to the summary page.

- Please let me know whether you found the clickthrough rate statistics that you were looking for. If not, I can send you a referral.

- Remember our free Bounce Rate workshop tomorrow night, at 6-8 PM, downtown Hyatt Regency, Debussy conference room. I hope that you can join us.

```
I'll be traveling for the next week. If you can't reach
me, you can call my assistant, Tammy, in my office at
212-555-8877.

I enjoyed seeing you the other day and I look forward
to working with you.

All the best,

Bob
```

The important content is now clearly visible at the top of the revised email. To get your point across quickly and respect the recipient's time, start with the most important information and put the small talk at the end (which is the reverse of what most senders actually do). The first sentence or two might appear as a preview in the recipient's inbox, so they can see those lines without opening the email. Those lines should be your call to action, not chit-chat.

Formatting the Body. In general, assume that your recipients use plain text email—that is, unadorned text without formatting, colors, special characters, or specific fonts. If you apply formatting, use a common system sans serif font, such as Arial or Verdana, at an easy-to-read font size of about 12 points. For lists, it's safest to use hyphens (-) instead of formatted bullets (•), so that these characters are visible no matter what the recipient's email settings are.

Tip: The excessive use of formatting and color (particularly the color red) increases the likelihood that your email will be flagged as spam and redirected to a spam folder, where it will sit unread.

Following Up with Nonresponders

Knowing how and when to follow up on an email increases the likelihood of getting a response from the recipient.

If you don't receive a response to your original email, then it's possible that your request was unclear. Use the guidelines in "The Message Body" on page 89 to ensure that your request is easy to read and appears at the beginning of your message.

Following up with a nonresponder—particularly after a missed deadline—can be tricky. You don't yet know the reason why there was no response, so suppress your frustration and be polite. Use "Please" and "Thank you," don't assign blame, and avoid harsh language. In general, expect longer response times via email because email communication implies lower urgency than text messages, telephone calls, and face-to-face conversations.

Some people check their email many times a day, whereas others may check only once a day at most. If your request can't wait two days, then follow up with a telephone call instead. If your request isn't urgent, allow at least two days for an email response (most of the time, responses take much less than 48 hours). After two days, it's acceptable to send a follow-up email, which can be formal or casual depending on your relationship with the recipient.

In the example email below, you can either forward the original email with the follow-up message at the top, or paste a copy of the original request (including the date and time stamp) below the follow-up message. Summarize the main points from the original request so that the recipient can see quickly which information you're waiting for.

Hi Judy,

I know that your inbox is probably full. I just wanted to make sure that you received my email the other day about our Customer Acquisition Cost workshop. The original email is copied below for quick reference. A summary:

- The workshop addresses some specific issues that you've mentioned.

- The workshop takes place at our downtown offices at 6-8 PM (snacks provided).

Please let me know if you have any questions.

All the best,

Bob

If your need is urgent and you either can't call or must escalate the request, then consider including the project manager or the recipient's boss in the email. However, be cautious when doing so because including a person's boss can cause hurt feelings, trouble for the recipient, and unforeseen consequences. If you truly need a response, and if the recipient is really the right person to ask, then make sure that there's no other way to get a timely answer.

Email offers several features for managing multiple recipients:

- **Cc.** To include a secondary recipient in an email, you can Cc them. Cc stands for carbon copy. When you send an email, the address of the main recipient is listed in the To field. You can use the Cc field to enter the address of anyone who should receive a copy of the email but isn't the person to whom you're directing the email. The person listed in the To field will see that the person in the Cc field also received a copy.

- **Bcc.** To send a copy of an email to a person without disclosing who else is copied, use Bcc, which stands for blind carbon copy. The recipient of an email can see any email address in the To and Cc fields, but can't see any addresses in the Bcc field. You can use the Bcc field to send a group email to a mailing list, for example, while protecting the privacy of the group members. Use Bcc with caution. If any one of the recipients clicks Reply All, then *everyone* will receive the reply. In some cases, it's better to forward the original email separately rather than use Bcc. Also, some people view the use of Bcc as mildly unethical because the original recipient (To address) is deliberately kept unaware of others involved in the email communication. Note also that some email programs add the label "undisclosed recipients" to the To line to show that Bcc has been used.

- **Reply All.** Use Reply All only when the entire group must receive your response. If only the original sender needs your reply, use Reply. The careless use of Reply All clutters the inboxes of group recipients with irrelevant replies.

Tip: Apply these guidelines to your own email responses. Many people expect a response no more than a day or two after sending an email. Try to at least send a confirmation receipt within 24 hours if you can't reply completely to the message.

How to Reply

Here are some tips for replying to email:

- **Best for non-urgent use.** Email generally isn't appropriate for urgent issues because email communication by its very nature implies that the content isn't urgent and can be attended to within 24 to 48 hours in general. Use email for non-urgent information, requests, and brief conversations. Email works best for sending files, communicating within a group, delegating tasks, and sending written communication.

- **No lectures or long conversations.** Email is a poor choice for information that requires a lot of explanation or a back-and-forth conversation. A telephone call is much faster and clearer than sending a long email or generating a long thread of replies, which is usually inefficient (and possibly rude).

- **Don't attach large files.** Large attachments download slowly and consume excessive space on the recipient's mail server. Instead, send links to large files that are stored on a shared network server or a cloud storage service such as Dropbox or Google Drive.

- **Don't send executable files.** Don't send a file that can be perceived as a threat. Files with the extensions .exe, .vbs, .bat, and .com are often used to spread viruses and other malware. In any case, antivirus programs and spam filters will block these attachments or redirect them to a spam folder (even if they're contained in a ZIP archive), so your recipient may not even receive them. If you do need to send a file that has one of these extensions, use a shared storage location and let the recipient know the file's purpose and source.

- **Don't be sarcastic.** The vocal variety of speech is absent in email, so a carelessly worded message can be easily misinterpreted. Avoid sarcasm in particular, which often comes across as offensive rather than witty or harsh. Before sending your email, re-read it, consider the ways that it can be misinterpreted, and then fix any ambiguities.

- **Respect cultural differences.** Every culture has its social conventions. When addressing people in another region or country, take pains to understand their norms and expectations, so that you don't offend them unintentionally.

- **Acronyms and emoji.** Don't use acronyms, such as LOL and BTW, in professional correspondence unless you've established a casual relationship with your recipient. Don't use obscure acronyms that the recipient might need to look up. Emoji, which are the smiley faces and other inline images, can also be seen as unprofessional in a business setting.

- **The ghost of emails past.** Treat all email as a permanent written record that can be shared easily and stored indefinitely. Don't send information via email that you wouldn't want to be made public or used against you. To avoid legal issues, human-resources problems, and other matters, never send anything confidential, sensitive, damaging, embarrassing, or illegal via email. It's better to talk face-to-face instead.

- **Respect people's time.** Be sure that your recipient wants to receive what you send. Cluttering people's inboxes with spam, chain letters, political screeds, and other low-content junk shows poor taste and is often seen as rude.

- **Proofread and spell-check.** Poor grammar and spelling makes you look unprofessional (or dumb). Always proofread and spell-check your emails manually. Don't rely solely on AutoCorrect, which often chooses the wrong word and can render your message unintentionally comic, offensive, or confusing.

- **Don't shout.** Be careful when using ALL UPPERCASE LETTERS, which is interpreted as shouting in electronic communications.

- **Complete the "To" field last.** To prevent sending an email accidentally before you review it, don't add any addresses to the "To" field until you're ready to send the message.

- **Calm down, write, send.** Never send an email when you're angry. After you hit Send, it's usually impossible to cancel delivery. If you write an emotionally charged email, don't send it until after you've calmed down and can re-read and edit it.

Acknowledging Incoming Emails. If you receive an email that you won't be able to fully respond to within 24 hours, it's polite to send an acknowledgement and let the sender know when you'll reply. In response to a long email with several requests, for example, you can respond like this:

> Dear Mrs. Alvarez,
>
> Thank you for your email regarding the Bounce Rate workshop needs. I'm in meetings all day today, but will look over your request tomorrow morning and answer your questions by the end of the day.
>
> All the best,
>
> Bob Clay

This acknowledgement repeats the important points of the original email and gives a time when the sender can expect a response. As a result, the sender knows when to follow up again if no response is received.

Using Autoresponders

You can use an autoresponder to let senders know that you're away from your email for a few days or weeks. An autoresponse is a reply sent automatically to any new incoming messages. You can set up autoresponses within your email settings or options. All modern email applications and services support autoresponders, which are also called automatic replies, vacation responders, out-of-office responders, and so on.

When you set up your autoresponder, choose the option to limit the reply to one per email address (this feature, if available, might be turned on by default). This way, if you receive more than one email from the same address, then the sender will be sent only one automated reply. This feature is also useful if you receive bulk mailings such as newsletters and promotional offers.

An autoresponse email should have most of the same elements as any other email. Properly used, autoresponders convey respect for the sender and set expectations for your eventual response. Let's improve the following autoresponse:

```
Thank you for contacting me. I am out of the office on
a trip to Maui this week. While I am away, Tina will be
able to help you.
```

In an autoresponse, state the actual dates that you'll be away from email to eliminate confusion over when your absence began and when the sender can expect a response. Instead of "this week," use:

```
I am away from my email from Monday, June 6th, through
Monday, June 13th.
```

If you don't plan to respond to emails within 24 hours of your return, list the date when the sender can expect a response:

```
I will respond to my messages within 48 hours of my
return.
```

or

```
I will respond to your message by the end of the day
Wednesday, June 15th.
```

Autoresponses with exact dates let the sender determine when to follow up or, if a response is needed sooner, ask someone else for help.

In a business setting, don't include much (if any) personal information in your autoresponse. Don't include where you'll be unless it applies directly to your business. If you're attending an industry conference, you might want to state that. But mentioning a vacation in Hawaii is unprofessional and smacks of gloating. It's also a personal security risk—you don't want everyone who happens to send you an email to know that your house is empty during that week.

Also, it's helpful to include a contact who can help the sender while you're away. If you mention someone who can help, include that person's:

- Email address

- Telephone number

- First and last name

- Company title

These details let the sender know your colleague's position in the company and relationship to you, making it easier to request assistance. Let your colleague know that you're sharing their contact information before you set up your autoresponse.

By applying these guidelines to the example autoresponse above, we get:

> Thank you for contacting Bob Clay at Dunham & Fry content marketing.
>
> I am away from my email from Monday, June 6th, through Monday, June 13th. I will respond to your message by the end of the day Wednesday, June 15th.
>
> If you have an urgent issue, please contact Tina Kelly, my administrative assistant, at 212-555-8888 or by email at tina.kelly@DunhamAndFry.com.
>
> Thank you,
>
> Bob Clay

Text Messages

Message Content

Texting in business is a relatively new type of communication compared with letters and email, and so the rules of etiquette are still changing.

Still, widely agreed-upon guidelines exist, many of which apply equally to text messages and email.

- **Check first.** Text messaging is the most familiar and casual form of communication in the workplace, so not everyone is comfortable using text for business purposes. Check first with your contact before using text messages for business.

- **Establish a degree of formality.** Decide how formal your text messages should be by assessing how casual your relationship with your contact is. Err on the side of too formal rather than too casual.

- **Keep it short.** Texting is intended for short messages. Some mobile phones break long text messages (>160 characters) into multiple parts that might not be displayed contiguously on the recipient's screen, possibly confusing the recipient. In other words, incoming messages from other senders might be displayed between the parts of your message. Texting works best for asking quick questions or passing on bits of information. Anything longer than a few sentences probably merits an email or telephone call.

- **More urgent than email.** Texting, despite being a more casual form of communication than email, carries a higher level of urgency. You can usually expect a response to a text within 12 hours. If your request requires an immediate response, make a telephone call or speak face-to-face instead.

- **Identify yourself initially.** If your telephone number isn't saved in your recipient's contacts list, then your recipient might not be able to identify who sent the text message. When you text someone for the first time, identify yourself with your full name and provide some context. This practice lets your recipient save your contact information and avoids awkward replies like "Who is this?" For example:

> Hi Sara, this is Tom Fisher. I'm a new hire in the accounting department. Our manager, Paul Foster, introduced us earlier this week. Are you available

this afternoon for about 10 minutes for some budgeting questions?

- **Be discreet.** People's phones often display the full text of incoming messages as notifications, meaning that not only can the recipient see your text but also anyone nearby. In a work environment, don't send anything confidential or embarrassing.

- **No sensitive information.** As with email, treat all text messages as a permanent written record that can be shared easily and stored indefinitely. Don't send information via text that you wouldn't want to be made public or used against you. To avoid legal issues, human-resources problems, and other matters, never send anything confidential, damaging, embarrassing, or illegal via text. Speak face-to-face instead.

- **No spam.** Never send spam (unsolicited advertising or marketing info) via a text message.

- **Spelling counts.** Grammar, spelling, and punctuation rules apply to all written business communication, including text messages. Even though texting is a more casual type of communication in business, it still requires complete sentences, correct grammar, and accurate spelling.

Don't send this:

> Hi Kate, Im runing late 4 the meeting. B there in 10.

Send this:

> Hi Kate, I'm running late for the meeting. I'll be there in 10 minutes.

- **Acronyms and emoji.** Although acronyms such as LOL and emoji (smiley faces and other inline images) are more acceptable in text messages than in email, establish a casual relationship with your recipient before using them. As with email, don't use obscure acronyms or symbols that the recipient might need to look up.

- **Proofread.** When typing text messages quickly on a small keyboard and display, it's easy to mistype words or fail to notice when AutoCorrect chooses the wrong word. Proofread your message for accuracy and tone before sending.

- **Acknowledge incoming messages.** Depending on the settings on your phone and the sender's phone, the sender might be able to see whether you've read the text message. If you receive and read a text message but can't fully reply immediately, then send an acknowledgement. For example:

  > I received your message. I can't respond fully now but I'll get back to you by the end of today.

Replies and Follow-Ups

- People generally expect a quick response to a text message, so try to reply within 12 hours.

- Wait 12 hours to follow up with someone who hasn't responded to your message, and be specific about which message you're referring to.

  Don't send this:

  > Did you get my message?

  Send this:

  > Tom, did you receive my message about the room change for the 3PM meeting today?

- As with email, be polite when following up. Use "Please" and "Thank you." For casual relationships, you can abbreviate "Thank you" as "TY". If you require an immediate response, make a telephone call or speak face-to-face instead.

- Accident statistics show that driving, operating machinery, and performing focused tasks can be dangerous while texting. Never distract yourself during these activities by texting. A newer but not yet widespread trend lets you respond to an incoming text by replying with only the single letter X. The X tells the sender that you're driving or unavailable and you'll respond later.

Telephone Calls

Answering and Making a Call

You've no doubt participated in enough awkward calls to know how tone of voice, background noise, and wait times can degrade conversations. A few basic practices can ensure that your calls convey the intended message.

The first impression that the caller receives comes from your tone of voice, starting from the moment that you answer the call. You've probably heard greetings like:

> *"Thank you for calling Lone Pine Winery. This is Cindy. How can I help you?"*

Such greetings are often delivered in a rapid or perfunctory way by a voice in a lower register with vocal monotony. You might get the impression that your call is unwanted because you're interrupting or annoying Cindy.

Don't be a Cindy. You can follow a few guidelines to create a call that's welcoming, productive, and efficient. In time, you may find that your own calls are answered and returned faster because the person knows they'll have a good experience.

- **Smile and slow down.** To make a caller feel welcome, before picking up a ringing phone, pause, take a breath, and then smile. Smiling tends to raise your voice to a higher register and add vocal variety. (It doesn't matter that the caller can't see your face.) If you keep a mirror on your desk, then you can use it to ensure that you smile as you talk. Also, slow your speech and enunciate. The caller will understand you better, will see that you're making time for them, and feel that their call actually *is* important.

- **Greeting content.** The actual content of the example greeting above works well. It includes the organization's name and the name of the person answering the call. Identifying yourself when answering a call puts the caller at ease and starts the conversation on a more personal level. The "How can I help you?" invites the caller to ask for help or state their own name.

- **Caller names and titles**. After you've greeted the caller, refer to them by name. If they don't introduce themselves, then you can ask a question like, "May I ask who I'm speaking to?" If you know the caller personally or if the caller tells you only their first name, then refer to them by their first name only. Otherwise, use the more formal Mr., Mrs., Ms., or Miss salutation until instructed differently. If the caller has a distinguished title, such as Doctor, Professor, or Judge, then use that title throughout the conversation. Note that addressing a caller by name adds a personal touch but sounds insincere when overused.

- **Three rings**. When answering a call, try to answer by the third ring. Often, when you hear the third ring, the caller's actually hearing their fourth ring. Too many rings might make a caller feel anxious that their call won't be answered.

When you're the caller, follow the same guidelines:

- Pause, take a breath, and then smile before dialing.

- When the call is answered, introduce yourself immediately or the receiver may start wondering whether you're soliciting or an unwanted caller. By introducing yourself first, you put the receiver at ease and they can relax and listen to you.

- Be brief. If your call might last more than a minute or two, then ask, "Is this a good time for you to talk?" This question lets the receiver prepare for a longer call or tell you a better time to call back.

- When ending a call, thank the person for their time. You can also repeat any action items that were agreed upon during the call. For example, "Thank you, Kim, for taking the time to talk with me. I'll email you that workshop description before the end of the day."

Leaving a Voicemail Message

Leaving the right voicemail message can make the difference between a call returned quickly and one returned slowly (or never). Let's improve the following voicemail message, which would likely not figure high on the list of calls to return:

"Um ... Yeah. This is Connie. You can call me at 212-555-3232. Thanks."

Proper voicemail etiquette lends you a professional and confident image before you've even spoken to the person on the phone. You can follow a few guidelines that will increase your chances of getting a quick response, boost your call's priority, and show respect for the receiver's time:

- **Prepare.** Before you call, know what you want to say in the event that you reach voicemail. Knowing what to say increases the effectiveness of your message and reduces er's, um's, and other filler words.

- **Slow down.** When leaving a message, speak clearly and slowly. A receiver who can't understand you can't return your call. Rushing also makes the receiver listen to your message multiple times to gather your contact information so they can return the call.

- **Smile.** Like any other telephone call, pause, take a breath, and then smile. The tone of your voice will express an elevated mood and attitude.

- **Repeat crucial info.** Recite the most important information twice. Begin your message with your full name. If you haven't spoken to the receiver before, then say how you know them or learned about them, and then leave your telephone number slowly and clearly. To end your message, repeat your full name and telephone number.

- **Keep it short, but not too short.** The example voicemail above is too short because it omits crucial information. But a long rambling message gives the receiver the impression that a returned call might likely result in a long conversation—they'll probably put off returning your call until they have time to talk, which might be much later in their day.

- **Be specific.** Tell the receiver why you're calling. A generic call-me-back message that leaves the reason for the call a mystery causes unease in the receiver, who can't prepare to return the call. Always state briefly what you would like to talk about.

- **List times to call back.** You've probably played phone tag, where both parties leave message after message for each other. If your schedule limits your availability to accept a returned call, then include the best times to reach you in your message.

- **Be polite.** Use "Please" and "Thank you." Shortened phrases like "Thanks" are appropriate only for family and close friends. If in doubt, always end the message with "Thank you."

By applying these guidelines to the example voicemail above, we get:

> *"Good afternoon. This is Connie Travers. My number is 212-555-3232. I found your information on your website and I'd like to talk to you about scheduling an advertising strategy meeting. You can reach me after 4 P.M. today or tomorrow between 9 and 12. Again, my name is Connie Travers and my number is 212-555-3232. Thank you.*

The revised message is more welcoming and specific, respects the receiver's time, and is more likely to be returned promptly during the preferred times.

If you don't receive a return call within 48 hours, feel free to leave a second message by following the same guidelines. Assume that a problem on the receiver's end kept them from returning your call. Leave a clear and polite message. Never imply guilt or express negative emotions.

Creating a Voicemail Greeting

Your own voicemail greeting reflects your business image and may be the first impression that your callers receive. Business can be won or lost on the content and tone of a voicemail greeting. Consider how the following impersonal greeting would leave a caller cold:

> *Thank you for calling Lone Pine Winery. We can't take your call right now but your call is important to us. Did you know you can communicate with us online? You can find us on the web at lonepinewinery.com.*

Please listen carefully because our menu options have changed. To speak to our sales department, press one. To speak to our shipping department, press two. To speak to our accounting department, press three. To speak to our legal department, press four. To leave a general voicemail, press five. Thank you and have a nice day.

You can follow a few guidelines to create a voicemail greeting that's welcoming and efficient:

- **Phone trees.** In general, never use a phone tree ("press one if... press two if...") unless it's necessary. Phone trees tell the caller that they're one of many callers and their issues aren't important. If a phone tree is necessary, it should have no more than three options at the first level, one of which is the option to speak to a live person. A second level of options, if it exists, should also have no more than three options, with a live person being one of them. Place the most common choice first in the list. If most of your callers want to speak to the retail department, then make that the first option they hear.

- **Clichés.** Avoid clichés such as "your call is important to us" or "our menu options have changed." These trite phrases are so overused that they now induce contrary emotions in the caller. If their call was truly important, then a human would have answered it.

- **Message length.** The example voicemail greeting above is too long. The caller's frustration grows with the time that it takes to wait for a message to finish.

Leaving a proper voicemail greeting can help you give a first impression of professional competence that sets the tone for future conversations. Here's a voicemail greeting that conveys neither warmth nor caring:

Hi. I'm out of the office today because my son's home sick from school. Please leave a message and I'll get back to you at my earliest convenience.

Here are some fixes for this greeting:

- **Smile**. Messages like these are often delivered in a hurried pace or harried tone. Pause, take a breath, and then smile before recording a voicemail greeting.

- **Omit personal details**. The caller doesn't want to know why you're out of the office. They want to know how to get their needs satisfied.

- **Include contact info**. Include the full name and department or organization of the person checking this voicemail, so that the caller doesn't wonder whether they've reached the right person's voicemail.

- **Include callback info**. State when the caller is likely to get a return call and how to get help if their matter is urgent.

By applying these guidelines to the example voicemail greeting above, we get a welcoming voicemail greeting that conveys a professional image and places the caller at ease:

Hello, you've reached Deena Moore with Lone Pine Winery. I'm sorry I missed your call. I'm out of the office today, Monday, May 16th, with no access to my voicemail. If this is an urgent matter, you can reach my assistant, Mona Garcia, at 707-555-4545. Otherwise, I will return your call first thing Tuesday morning, when I return. Thank you for your patience.

What to Say, Where, and When

Telephone calls, like all forms of communication, have rules of etiquette that accord respect to the person you're speaking to and others around you. Each country and region has different rules, but here are some do's and don'ts within the United States that set the tone for present and future conversations:

- **Find the right place**. Make or answer calls from an appropriate place to talk. If you're speaking on a mobile phone, respect the people around you as well as the person on the other end of the line. It's inappropriate to have telephone conversations in restaurants, coffee shops, bookstores, libraries, and public bathrooms, in lines (queues), and in places where people go to concentrate, work, or relax. Silence your phone or set it to vibrate-only in these locations to respect the people around you. If you take a call, quietly and quickly excuse yourself and go outside or to an appropriate place before you answer your phone.

- **Lower your voice.** Speak at a respectful volume. The people around you don't want to hear your conversation.

- **One conversation at a time.** Always give the other caller your full attention. Never hold a telephone conversation when you're also speaking or interacting face-to-face with someone else. Talking on the phone while you're making a purchase in a store, for example, is rude to the clerk who's trying to help you and usually irritates the caller, who can tell that you're distracted.

- **Focus.** If you can't dedicate your full attention to the caller, then call back when you can. Although you might not realize it, multitasking while you talk comes across in your voice. To the other person, you sound distracted or uninterested in what they're saying. You've probably had a telephone conversation in which the other person's focus suddenly shifted away from you, accompanied by a change in vocal tone and a quick goodbye like "Uh, it was nice talking to you. I'll call you later, OK?"

- **Minimize background noise.** Turn off the TV or radio. Roll up the car windows. Don't type on a keyboard. Don't eat. Don't talk to other people in the room. Make sure that children and pets can't be overheard.

- **Declare long silences.** A long silence can put the other person on edge. If you need to put the caller on mute for a moment, or if you need a quiet moment to think before responding, then let them know beforehand. A sudden long silence can leave the other caller wondering whether you're distracted or the call was dropped. Put the other person at ease by prefacing a long silence with a simple phrase like, "Can you hold one moment while I ask my colleague?" or "Just a moment, I want to think this through before I respond."

- **Be discreet.** Remember that there could be someone else listening to your telephone conversation without your knowledge. Treat every business call like a permanent record—if you wouldn't write it in an email or letter, then you shouldn't say it on a telephone call. Whenever possible, save delicate information for a face-to-face conversation.

Business Letters

Letter Content

The business letter is one of the oldest forms of business communication and has well-defined rules of etiquette and structure. When you write a business letter, many of the same cautions and rules of email apply. Because a business letter is the most formal mode of business communication, it's essential to format it correctly and use the proper degree of formality.

- **Urgency.** A letter sent via standard postal service delivery conveys a high level of formality but a low level of urgency. To increase a letter's perceived urgency, send it via an alternate form of expedited delivery such as an overnight service, courier, or hand delivery.

- **Content.** A business letter is most appropriate for formal or important content, such as legal matters or sensitive topics that require documentation. For quick or conversational messages, use email or text. For personal or emotionally charged matters, make a telephone call, where vocal intonation can convey the right message.

- **Tone.** The vocal variety of speech is absent in written communication, so a carelessly worded or sarcastic letter can be easily misinterpreted. Before sending your letter, re-read it, consider the ways that it can be misinterpreted, and then fix any ambiguities.

- **Politeness.** As the most formal type of business communication, a letter requires polite language. Use (but don't overuse) "Please" and "Thank you" when the situation calls for it.

- **Grammatical correctness**. Misspellings and grammatical errors are conspicuous, signify poor attention to detail, and diminish the importance of your message.

- **Permanence**. Never send any information in any form of written communication that's illegal or that you wouldn't want to be made public or used against you. Treat every letter as a permanent and public written record. After you send it, it leaves your control—it can be copied, scanned, shared, and stored easily.

Formatting a Business Letter

A properly formatted business letter conveys formality, professionalism, and gravity. Let's improve the following business letter.

Dear Mrs. Jones,

It has come to my attention that your account is past due. Please remit payment to our office as soon as possible to avoid late fees.

Sincerely,

Tom Foley

The sender's name and address (required). Begin with your name and address. This information lets the recipient quickly see who the letter is from and where to send a reply if one is needed.

The date (required). Skip a line after the sender's name and address and insert the date, which helps you and the recipient refer back to the letter at a later date.

The recipient's name and address (optional). Skip a line after the date and insert the recipient's full name and address or only their name, title, and department. This field is also called the inside address. If you like, you can omit this field entirely.

The greeting (required). A greeting can take many forms. In a formal letter like the example above, end the greeting with a colon (:) instead of a comma (,). Use a comma for personal letters, including thank-you notes, sympathy cards, and other casual correspondence. Here are some rules of thumb for using salutations in the greeting and body of a letter:

- If you don't know the recipient personally, then use a standard salutation (Mr., Ms., Mrs., or Dr.) and the last name.

- If the recipient is a longtime client, a coworker, a friend, or someone that you know personally, then you can use only the first name (Dear Janet:).

- If you don't know a woman's preferred salutation, then use the salutation Ms. rather than Miss or Mrs.

- If you don't know the recipient's gender, then use either the full first name or initials rather than a salutation (Dear D. F. Jones:).

- If you don't know the recipient's name, then use their title (Dear Vice President of Sales:) or use To Whom It May Concern:

- Always abbreviate Mr., Ms., Mrs., and Dr. Write out most other titles: Professor, Judge, Governor, and Reverend, for example.

The subject line (optional). The subject line is an optional summary of the topic of the letter. It begins with the word Subject and a colon (:) and is placed between the greeting and body. The subject line is typically only a few words, and no more than a line or two.

The body (required). You can start with some polite filler but get to the point quickly. Explain the situation in brief paragraphs and make your request or response in a straightforward, concise way. Avoid slang and legalese. If you have a personal relationship with the recipient, you can add a final, personal sentence, such as "Give my best to Ken." Single-space the paragraphs, but leave double spaces between one paragraph and the next. Include specific information and descriptions that identify the subject. The example letter above mentions that the account is past due and requests payment but fails to state what payments are past due and how much to remit.

The close (required). The letter's close depends on the context of the letter and your relationship with the recipient. If you have a personal relationship with the recipient, then close with "Best wishes" or "Regards". For general business purposes, close with "Sincerely" or "Yours truly" or "Cordially". Don't close with a presumptive phrase like "Thank you in advance". Closing with "Respectfully" is too formal unless you're writing to a high-status recipient. In any case, standard closes rarely hint at actual feeling.

Your typed name (required). Skip three to four lines after the close and type your name as you intend to sign it. If you have a professional title or role that's relevant to the purpose of the letter, such as Assistant Manager or Lecturer, then add it directly below your name.

Your signature (required). Sign your name in blue or black ink. Match your signature to your typed name. A shorter signature is a sign of impatience.

Special notations (optional). Lowest on the page, always flush left, are notations that indicate the following circumstances if they are applicable:

cc: A. Davis *or* Copies to: A. Davis

> A "carbon copy" (photocopy or duplicate printout) is being sent simultaneously to interested party Davis. For multiple cc'd parties, list the names alphabetically, one per line:

cc: A. Davis
    B. Hunt

encl. *or* Enclosures (2)

> The mailing contains an enclosure (always mentioned in the body of the letter). A parenthesized number indicates how many pieces are enclosed.

TF: gsr *or* TF/gsr

> The writer (initials *TF*) has used the services of a typist (initials *gsr*). This notation is rarely used nowadays.

Typeface. For most letters, use a traditional serif typeface such as Palatino, Garamond, Caslon, Minion, or Times New Roman. For a modern feel, use a sans serif typeface such as Helvetica, Futura, Proxima Nova, or Arial. Set the font size between 10 and 12 points. Don't use monospaced, script, decorative, or novelty typefaces, which reduce the letter's formality and are often tiring to read.

Alternative formats. You can use block format (more formal) or modified block format (less formal) to arrange a business letter's elements on the page.

- **Block format.** All page elements are flush left. The first lines of paragraphs are not indented. "Flush left" means that the lines begin at the left margin.

- **Modified block format.** The sender's name and address, date, close, typed name, and signature are shifted toward the right margin. The recipient's name and address and special notations are flush left. The first line of every body paragraph is indented by ¼–½ inches (5–10 spaces). "Toward the right margin" means that the lines should end at or near the right margin.

Margins. Set the letter's margins to one inch on all sides. In Microsoft Word, for example, the Page Setup settings are:

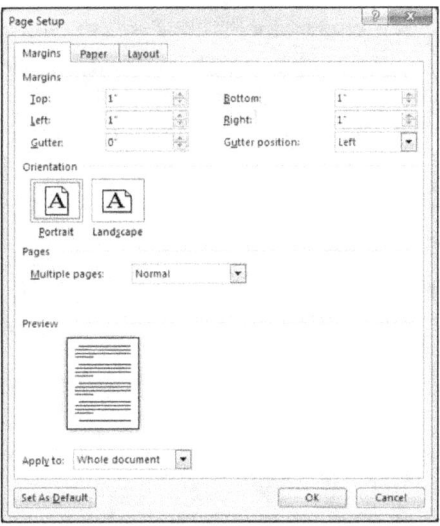

By applying these guidelines to the example business letter above and using block format, we get:

Tom Foley
Landry & Thomas
123 Elm Street
Chicago, IL 60605

May 25, 2020

Ms. Patricia Jones
Vice President
The Rookery
987 Granite Avenue
Boulder, CO 80304

Ms. Jones:

Subject: Account past due

Our records show that we have not yet received payment on your two most recent invoices numbered 1055 and 1064. I have enclosed copies of these invoices for your convenience. The total outstanding balance is $885.32.

Please send your payment to our main office at 123 Elm Street, Chicago, IL 60605 as soon as possible to avoid incurring the $60 late fee.

If you need any assistance or have questions, you can reach me at 312-555-4455.

Sincerely,

Tom Foley
Enclosures (2)

Personal Business Letters and Cards

In a culture of deals and transactions, writing personal cards and notes shows your intimate side and increases your chances of being remembered. Here are some general guidelines for writing greeting cards, thank-you notes, sympathy cards, and thinking-of-you notes:

- **Use a pen.** It's more respectful and caring to handwrite personal messages.

- **Keep it simple.** Write in plain, heartfelt prose. Short messages are often more effective and appreciated than long ones.

- **Sign your full name.** Sign your first and last name, especially for sympathy cards and other occasions where the recipient is likely to receive many cards. Your full name ensures that the recipient knows who the card's from.

Sympathy Cards. The following guidelines apply to sympathy cards:

- **Don't delay.** Send a sympathy card as soon as you hear of the death.

- **What not to write.** *I know how you feel. She's in a better place now. You'll feel better in time. At least he went quickly.* These stock phrases may be well-intentioned but they're more likely to irritate the grieving recipient.

- **Avoid religious references.** Don't mention religion unless you know with certainty the beliefs of both the deceased and the recipient.

- **Offering help.** If you offer help, then state a specific and appropriate way that you or your business can assist. Avoid the general, *Call me if you need anything.*

- **Addressing the family.** If you knew the deceased but not the family, then address the card to the closest family member, typically the widow, widower, or eldest child.

- **Include a personal memory.** If you knew the deceased well, then you can include a brief memory or story with your message.

If you're at a loss for what to write, a combination of generic phrases will usually suffice:

He'll be truly missed.

I was very sad to hear of Jane's death.

I'm very sorry to hear of your loss.

Please let me know whether I can help you by picking up groceries or running errands.

Jim will always be in our hearts.

Kelly brought us joy every day.

Please know that you are in my thoughts.

She was always kind and her smile lit up any room.

There are no words to tell you how sorry I am.

You are in my thoughts during this difficult time.

You are in my thoughts.

Thank-You Notes. Thank-you notes are seldom sent these days, but a simple act of gratitude can improve your image and set you apart from the competition. The following guidelines apply to thank-you notes:

- **If in doubt, send.** It's best to err on the side of formality rather than inadvertently offend someone by failing to send a handwritten thank-you note.

- **Don't delay.** Send a thank-you note immediately after the event. Write and mail the note by the end of the next day.

- **The greeting.** Open with the recipient's first name.

- **The body.** State what you're thankful for. If the thank-you is following a business transaction, then mention a personal or positive moment from the meeting. If it's a gift, then mention what the gift was and how it will affect you.

- **The close.** End with a polite close such as "Sincerely" or "Best regards".

Here are some examples of appropriate thank-you notes:

Thank you so much for the Star Wars coffee mug. I'll begin each morning (and afternoon!) with it.

I really appreciate the donation that you made to The Otter Fund. Your generosity will help us protect the sea otter and its habitat. You have truly made a difference.

Thank you so much for all your hard work as we rebuilt my antique wine press yesterday. I loved hearing your stories about your grandfather and seeing the beautiful photos of the old vineyard. Thank you for sharing that with me.

5 Advanced Google Searches

Efficient online research is a crucial skill for marketers. Google's simple interface hides a lot of power. With a few simple tricks, you can find what you're looking for quickly and accurately. Applying Google's special operators and other countermeasures to your searches prevents overly broad results flooded with ads, web spam, mirror sites, link farms, content farms, and other low-quality websites. Almost all these techniques work for other search engines, such as Bing, Duck Duck Go, and Startpage.com.

Search for Multiple Words
A one-word search won't yield targeted results. Start with a short multiple-word search. If the results are still too broad, add words and search operators (page 128) to get fewer, but more-relevant, results.

Tip: Google limits queries to 32 words.

Compare the front-page results and total number of results of these increasingly specific searches:

> mesothelioma
>
> mesothelioma lawyer
>
> mesothelioma lawyer chicago
>
> mesothelioma lawyer chicago free consultation

Case Doesn't Matter

Searches are case insensitive. Uppercase or capitalized search terms return the same results as lowercase terms. You can't direct Google to respect case differences. These pairs of searches give the same results:

> Aspen CO hotels *and* aspen co hotels

> cia coups *and* CIA coups

Tip: A few exceptions to the case rule: search operators (page 128) such as site: and filetype: must be lowercase, and the OR operator (page 126) must be uppercase.

Omit Stop Words

Stop words are common, typically short words that do little to narrow a search. Stop words include *a, an, at, how, i, in, is, of, on, the, to, where,* and *who.* Google ignores stop words in searches unless they're part of common names or phrases (for example, *the who, episode i, take that,* and *to be or not to be*).

Searches posed as questions—*how do i…, how many…, what is…, where can i …*—contain superfluous words that typically reduce the relevance of the results. The search

> female population china

is better than

> how many females are in china

because the latter contains words (like *many*) that probably don't appear in the most-relevant documents. Also, *population* is more descriptive than *how many.*

Quote Exact Phrases

To look for an **exact phrase** (rather than words scattered anywhere in a document), surround your keywords with quotes to make Google match the word order exactly. The unquoted search

> highest waterfalls

returns pages where the words appear in any order, anywhere on the page, whereas the quote-enclosed search

"highest waterfalls"

returns fewer (but more-useful) pages that contain the word *highest* followed immediately by the word *waterfalls*.

You can include multiple quoted phrases in the same search. The search

"highest waterfalls" "north america"

matches pages that contain *north america* before or after *highest waterfalls*, but favoring pages where *highest waterfalls* precedes *north america*.

You can mix quoted and unquoted phrases in the same search:

airborne "snake oil"

"highest waterfalls" campsites "north america"

Don't quote words that aren't natural phrases. The search

"highest waterfalls north america"

returns few or no results because the word order and usage is awkward in natural language.

Tip: If a particular search yields no results, Google will often instead return results for a search phrase that's similar to the original one. A message at the top of the results tells you what Google is actually searching for.

Be conservative. Google already accounts for word order and proximity, so quoted phrases might miss good results. The search

"john f kennedy"

misses pages that refer to *john kennedy* or *john fitzgerald kennedy*.

Tip: You can also use quotes to find exact terms (page 125).

See also "Find Verbatim Terms" on page 127.

Rearrange Search Words

The order of the words in your search affects the number of results and how they're ranked. Google favors pages whose word order matches that of your search phrase. These pairs of searches give different results:

> hot dog *vs.* dog hot

> beautiful stay *vs.* stay beautiful

> red white blue *vs.* white blue red

Swap Singular and Plural Forms

Consider whether the singular or plural forms of search words will improve your results.

> oil spill *vs.* oil spills

> hunting knife *vs.* hunting knives

> "london marathon" "runner up" *vs.* "london marathon" "runners up"

> french chateau *vs.* french chateaus *vs.* french chateaux

Use Wildcards for Unknown Words (* Operator)

The * (asterisk) is a **wildcard** character that lets you omit one or more words in a search. Google treats the wildcard as a placeholder for unknown term(s) and finds the best matches.

Wildcards can help you find:

- Products and services:

    microsoft *

- Names that you can't remember:

    * cathedral moscow

- Names that are commonly misspelled or have alternate spellings:

    * "circle theorem"

- Adjectives or modifiers:

  miami * cars

  The * stands in for rental, new, used, classic, Honda, red, and so on.

- Exact phrases:

  "ate * hot dogs in * seconds"

  Asterisks substitute for only entire words, not parts of words (*ing in las vegas won't work).

Tip: When * appears between two numbers, Google interprets it as the multiplication operator and displays the product of the two numbers. For example, *7 * 6.5.*

Specify a Range of Numbers (.. Operator)

To search for pages containing numbers in a specified range, use .. (two dots) between two numbers. The numbers can denote years, prices, shoe sizes, or any numerical measures. To search within a price range, use currency symbols (*blender 60* and *blender $60* give different results, for example). If you omit a range's upper limit, Google assumes it to be infinity (*50..* matches numbers greater than or equal to 50, for example). A missing lower limit is assumed to be zero. Don't add spaces between the dots and the numbers.

Here are some examples:

scorsese movies 1970..1979

bikes portland $800..$1200

stars within 50..250 light years

earthquakes 8.. magnitude

type ..2 civilizations

london properties £2000000..£5000000

Omit (Some) Punctuation

Google ignores lesser-used punctuation and special characters in search phrases, including ! ? , ; # ^ & * ( ) = [ ] /. For example, *kevorkian* and *kevorkian!* give the same results.

Google does *not* ignore punctuation in the following situations:

- Heavily used symbols: % $ \ . @ # +.

- Currency symbols that indicate prices ($1, £9.99, 5.000,00€, ¥18000).

- The @ character in an email address (president@whitehouse.gov).

- Punctuation in common terms (*AT&T, F# minor,* and *C++*).

- A hyphenated term matches the same term with a hyphen, without a hyphen, and with a space instead of a hyphen. The search term *year-end*, for example, matches *year-end, yearend,* and *year end;* and *e-mail* matches *e-mail, email,* and *e mail.* If you're not sure whether a word is hyphenated, then search for its hyphenated form.

- A word with an apostrophe (single quote, ') doesn't usually match the same word without an apostrophe. *i'll* doesn't match *ill,* for example, but *we're* matches *were.* Also, singular and plural possessive apostrophes give different results (*children's books* vs. *childrens' books*—the latter is equivalent to *childrens books*).

- Diacritical marks—accents, umlauts, tildes, and so on—matter (*internet café paris* and *internet cafe paris* give different results).

- Underscores (_) that connect words matter. Underscores are often used in programming identifiers: *max_int* and *__import__,* for example.

Exclude Terms (- Operator)

Precede each term that you *don't* want to appear in the results with a - (hyphen/minus sign). Don't add a space between the - and the term. The search

        lion -football -basketball -disney -os -cowardly

finds results for *lion* that omit sports figures, shows (Disney's *The Lion King*), Mac operating systems, and Oz residents.

You can use - in front of quoted phrases (page 120):

"merry men" -"robin hood"

And in front of some search operators (page 128):

parenting -site:ehow.com

Find Exact Terms (" Operator)

Surround each term that *must* appear in the results with quotes. The " operator is often used with stop words (page 120) that Google would otherwise ignore:

"the" rock

"the" "the" *(The The is a band)*

The " operator stops Google from using synonyms and word variants automatically (called **stemming**). The search

child car seat

matches *child, children, children's, car, cars, carseat, booster, seat,* and *seats*; whereas

"child" "car" "seat"

matches each word precisely as typed.

You can also use the " operator to find exact phrases (page 120).

Tip: The " operator replaced the + (plus) operator in late 2011.

See also "Find Verbatim Terms" on page 127.

Find Synonyms (~ Operator)

To find synonyms, precede a word with a ~ (tilde). Don't add a space between the ~ and the word. (The ~ key is located to the left of the 1 key on most keyboards.)

In the search

> ~cheap tickets

~cheap matches *discount, low cost, last minute, inexpensive, affordable,* and other synonyms.

In the search

> ~running shoes

~running matches *athletic, sports, track, marathon, run, runner's, runner,* and other synonyms.

See also "Find Verbatim Terms" on page 127.

Find Alternate Terms (OR Operator)

By default, Google returns only pages that match *all* your search terms. To find pages that contain *any* of your search terms, use the OR operator. Type *OR* in UPPERCASE or Google will interpret it as a search term rather than as an operator.

The search

> surfing australia OR hawaii

gives surfing results for *either* Australia or Hawaii, whereas the search

> surfing australia hawaii

gives surfing results that include *both* Australia and Hawaii on the same page.

OR applies to the search terms immediately adjacent to it; you can chain OR terms:

> big-wave surfing australia OR hawaii OR california

You can use OR with quoted phrases (page 120):

> filter "junk email" OR spam

You can substitute a | (vertical bar) for OR:

> big-wave surfing australia | hawaii | california

Unlike OR, the | symbol needn't be surrounded by spaces

big-wave surfing australia|hawaii|california

Tip: Google also has an AND operator, but it's implied by default so don't bother typing it. The exclusion operator isn't NOT, it's the minus sign (-, page 124). OR, AND, and - () are called **logical operators** or **boolean operators**.

Find Verbatim Terms

Google expands and improves your searches automatically by correcting spelling, substituting synonyms, and more. In some cases, those changes might not help you find what you're looking for, even if you use the quote operator (page 125) to find exact terms. To turn off the normal search improvements, you can turn on **verbatim** search: click "Tools" near the top of the Google results page, click "All results", and then click "Verbatim".

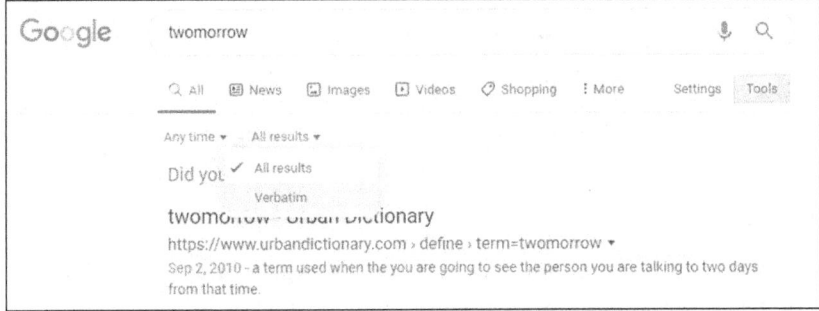

When verbatim search is turned on, Google *won't*:

- Correct misspelled terms

- Personalize searches by using previously visited sites and other personal information

- Include synonyms (page 125) of search terms

- Find results that match similar terms

- Stem search terms (like searching for *eating* when you type *eat*)

- Make some search terms optional

Use Search Operators

You can use **search operators** to limit results by web location, file type, and various metadata (title, link text, and so on). Operators must be typed in all lowercase letters and followed immediately by a : (colon).

site:

Use site: to search only a specified website (URL) or domain. Don't add a space after the ":".

Here are some examples:

site:apple.com *(all indexed pages on the site)*

iphone site:macrumors.com

interview -election site:wnyc.org/shows *(subdomain search)*

flu OR influenza epidemic OR pandemic site:.gov *(search only .gov sites)*

nietzsche schopenhauer course site:.ac.uk | site:.edu.au | site:.edu *(multiple-site search)*

aesthetics site:.jp *(the country code* jp *denotes Japan; standard country codes are listed at iana.org/domains/root/db)*

filetype:

Use filetype: to search for specific types of files by **filename extension** (the few characters after a filename's last dot). For example, you can restrict your search to Word documents, to Excel documents, to Power-Point files, or to PDF files by adding *filetype:doc, filetype:xls, filetype:ppt,* or *filetype:pdf,* respectively, to your search. Don't add a space after the ":".

Common filename extensions include:

- Image (.jpg/.jpeg, .gif, .bmp, .png, .webp, .svg)
- Video (.avi, .flv, .mov,. .mp4, .mkv, .mpg, .wmv)
- Audio (.mp3, .wav, .flac, .ogg, .wma)
- Adobe Flash (.swf)

- Portable Document Format (.pdf)

- PostScript (.ps)

- HTML (.htm/.html)

- CSS (.css)

- Word (.doc/.docx)

- Excel (.xls/.xlsx)

- PowerPoint (.ppt/.pptx)

- OpenDocument text (.odt/.fodt)

- OpenDocument spreadsheet (.ods/.fods)

- OpenDocument presentation (.odp/.fodp)

- Rich Text Format (.rtf/.wri)

- Text (.txt)

- XML (.xml)

Tip: If you search for webpages, note that not all URLs (web addresses) have the extension .html or .htm. Some pages (like https://www.google.com) have no extension, and others have an extension that doesn't match their actual file type.

You can also find source code. Filename extensions for common programming languages include:

- C/C++ (.c, .cc, .cpp, .cxx, .h, .hpp)

- C# (.cs)

- Go (.go)

- Java (.java)

- Javascript (.js)

- Objective-C (.m)

- Perl (.pl)

- PHP (.php)

- Python (.py)

- R (.r)

- Ruby (.rb)

- Swift (.swift)

- Visual Basic (.vb, .bas)

  Here are some examples:

  > confidential internal filetype:doc

  > banner ads filetype:swf *(Flash files)*

  > statistics ~help filetype:xlsx

  > quicksort filetype:c *(C source-code files)*

  > human population overshoot filetype:pdf

intitle:

Use intitle: to search for documents whose title contains the specified word or quoted phrase (page 120). A webpage's title appears in the page tab or the title bar of your browser. (Technically, it's the text specified by the <title> tag in the page's HTML source code.) On Google's main results page, the title is the (usually blue) hyperlinked text. Don't add a space after the ":".

Here are some examples:

> observatory intitle:haleakala

> intitle:cheating site:.edu

> intitle:"old faithful" site:nps.gov

> intitle:"evacuation plan" filetype:doc *(intitle: searches the text in the File > Properties dialog box of Microsoft Office documents)*

allintitle:

allintitle: works like intitle: but finds multiple words within titles. Add a space after the ":".

Here are some examples:

> allintitle: run excel macro site:microsoft.com

> allintitle: celebrate chinese new year

Putting intitle: in front of every word in your query is equivalent to putting allintitle: at the front of your query. The preceding example is the same as

> intitle:celebrate intitle:chinese intitle:new intitle:year

inurl:

Use inurl: to search for documents whose URL (web address) contains the specified word. Don't add a space after the ":".

Here are some examples:

> inurl:ftp site:stanford.edu

> excel inurl:support site:microsoft.com

allinurl:

allinurl: works like inurl: but finds multiple words within URLs. Add a space after the ":".

Here are some examples:

> allinurl: support edge site:microsoft.com *(Edge is Microsoft's web browser)*

> allinurl: emergency cdc disasters *(cdc stands for Centers for Disease Control)*

Putting inurl: in front of every word in your query is equivalent to putting allinurl: at the front of your query. The preceding example is the same as

> inurl:emergency inurl:cdc inurl:disasters

related:

Use related: to list webpages that are similar (according to Google) to a specified webpage. Don't add a space after the ":".

Here are some examples:

related:google.com

related:www.montereybayaquarium.org

Tip: You can also see similar pages by clicking the tiny ▼ button below a search result.

---

info:

Use info: to list some information that Google knows about the specified webpage, including a link to the page, the page's title, a snippet, a link to similar pages, and other odds and ends. Don't add a space after the ":".

Here are some examples:

info:http://www.nasa.gov/missions/

info:queenstown-nz.co.nz

Tip: You can also see page information by typing a URL (web address) directly into a Google search box.

---

link:

Use link: to list pages that have links pointing to the specified webpage. Don't add a space after the ":".

Here are some examples:

link:http://earthquake.usgs.gov/

link:news.bbc.co.uk

cache:

Use cache: to show a snapshot of the specified webpage as it looked when Google last examined it (which could have been seconds ago or months ago, depending on your timing and the popularity of the page—a message at the top of a cached page gives the page's age). You can use cache: to find old versions of webpages that have been deleted or edited. If you add words to the end of your query, those words will be highlighted on the cached page. The cache: operator works only if Google has downloaded its own copy of the page. Don't add a space after the ":".

Here are some examples:

cache:http://www.britishmuseum.org

cache:nps.gov/faqs.htm camping

Tip: You can also see a cached page by clicking the tiny ▼ button below a search result.

Index